MULTICULTURAL COMMUNICATION STRATEGIES

How To Be More Successful With:

- Customers
- Colleagues
- Community

JUDITH A. STARKEY

JAMS Publishing Co.
Chicago, Illinois, USA

MULTICULTURAL COMMUNICATION STRATEGIES
How To Be More Successful With: Customers, Colleagues, Community
by Judith A. Starkey

Copyright ©1996 by: The Starkey Group, Inc.

Printed and bound in the United States of America. All rights reserved. No part of this book may be reproduced or transmitted in any form or by any means, electronic or mechanical, including photocopying, recording, or by an information storage and retrieval system (except for brief quotation—not to exceed 100 words—in a review or professional work, with attribution to author) without permission in writing from the publisher.

Although the author has made every effort to ensure the accuracy and completeness of information contained in this book, we assume no responsibility for errors, inaccuracies, omissions, or any inconsistency herein. Any slights of people, places, or organizations are unintentional.

ISBN 0-9648686-0-1

Library of Congress Catalog Card No. 95-080413

ATTENTION CORPORATIONS, COLLEGES AND PROFESSIONAL ORGANIZATIONS: Quantity discounts are available on bulk purchases of this book for educational purposes or fund-raising. For information contact the publisher: JAMS Publishing Co., 333 West Wacker Drive, Suite 700, Chicago, IL 60606-1225, USA, Tel: 312 444 2025.

First Edition

To John S., for his continuing support in the face of seemingly insurmountable odds.

To my parents, for their lifelong examples of perseverance, survivorship and nonjudgmental love.

�֍   �֍   ✷

―――――――

✷   ✷   ✷

TABLE OF CONTENTS

Preface   v

Introduction   1
    USA Population Trends   2
    Quote: George Washington   4

1.   **The Meaning of Culture**   5
    Definition of Culture   5
    Cultural Tree of Life™   6
    Forces of Acculturation   7
    Cultural Change Factors   8
        Mixtures of Cultural Heritages   8
        Regional Differences   9
        Gender   9
        Age   10
        Education   10
        Personal Style   10
        Class Status   11
    Examples of Cultural Groups & Values   12
    Quote: Earl Shorris   14

TABLE OF CONTENTS

2. Multicultural Communication Model 15
Approach People As Individuals First 15
Listen, Observe and Clarify 17
Consider Cultural Heritages 21
    Male Dominance 21
    Individualism vs. Group 21
        Self-Reliance 25
    Religion 26
        Buddhism 26
        Christianity 26
        Confucianism 27
        Hinduism 27
        Islam 27
        Judaism 27
        Kwanzaa 27
    Authority/Hierarchy 28
    Filial Piety 29
    Language 30
    Self 31
    Saving Face 33
    Eye Contact 34
    Emotional Expression 35
    Smiling 37
    Touching 38
    Negotiating 38
    Time 39
    Space 39
    Reasoning 40
    Humor 41
    Work and Family 41
    Role of Personal Styles 42
        Individualistic 44
        Group 45

TABLE OF CONTENTS

Develop Dialogues & Relationships 46
With ESL People 46
Everyday Interactions 47
Quote: From Words of Will Rogers 50

3. **The Cultures of Gender**   **51**
Male Viewpoints 51
Female Viewpoints 53
Brain Differences 54
Acculturations 55
Gender Preferences 56
Communication Strategies 59
"Women in Business: A Cultural Change" 61
Quote: Gloria Steinem 67

4. **Cultural Compendium**   **69**

5. **The Multicultural U.S. Marketplace**   **77**
"A Growing Customer Focus: Cultural Diversity" 77
    Retail 78
    Computers 83
    Financials 83
    Automobiles 84
    Entertainment 85
"Multicultural Customer Relations" 88
    Case Study: Asian/Anglo Women 89
    Case Study: Hispanic/Black Men 91
General Recommendations 93
Quote: Jennie Tong 94

TABLE OF CONTENTS

6.   International Philosophies/Protocol   95
   USA 95
   International-General 97
   Europe 100
   Latin America 102
   Asia 105
   Middle East 110
   Quote: Tom Peters 112

7.   Afterword   113
   "Overcoming Our Need to Blame" 113
   "Unity from Diversity" 116
   Quote: Barbara Jordan 122

Glossary   123

Selected References   127

Response Request   149

*   *   *

Preface

The dynamics of interpersonal communication have intrigued me ever since childhood. At about the age of four I realized that people did not always say what they meant (a particularly frustrating puzzlement at that age) and miscommunication often occurred as a result. Sometimes the consequences were disastrous. This curious and often aggravating phenomenon gripped me and I've been trying to facilitate better communication among the peoples of the world ever since.

As I grew up and my work expanded, it seemed that many of the problems of the world stemmed from people not appreciating the complexities of why others say and do what they do. My convictions led me to career channels in network news broadcasting (USA and Europe), human resources management and development in the U.S. corporate sector (a diversified manufacturer and a major oil company) and, for most of the last decade, speaking, training and consulting in the private and public sectors. Case histories from these experiences, as well as those of others, are cited throughout the following chapters.

My journey, which began years ago in Indiana, has taken me around a large part of the globe. Today, however, many of the same global communication opportunities exist within U.S. borders. Indeed, increasing globalization is one of the catalysts for my writing this book.

I hope you will find the following pages helpful in *your* communication exchanges. If so, drop me a line or use the response form in the back of the book. The quest for improved communication techniques never ends. Your observations are most welcome, and I would enjoy hearing from you.

Bon communication!

Introduction

As we enter the 21st Century we find we are living in an increasingly closer global community. Centuries ago people on one side of the world had little information about those living on the other side. Thanks to today's technological advances, however, instantaneous world communication is possible.

With these advances has come the advent of a global economy, where countries are becoming interdependent upon each other for their financial stability. More and more companies are developing international joint ventures, investors are establishing outposts all over the world, and people emigrate in ever growing numbers to new lands of opportunity. Whereas in the past many countries had primarily homogeneous populations with a common cultural heritage, today more and more countries are finding their societies are becoming progressively diverse. These new cultural influences are having an impact on their national profile.

USA Population Trends

The USA is one of the most dramatic examples. Consider these actual population statistics from the U.S. Census Bureau as of September 1995:

YEAR 1995

74% - Non-Hispanic White
12% - African-American
10% - Hispanic
 3% - Asian-American
 1% - American Indian

Compare these figures with projections from the U.S. Census Bureau indicating that by the year 2050 the American population will be about evenly divided between non-Hispanic whites and other population groups:

YEAR 2050

53% - Non-Hispanic White
21% - Hispanic
15% - African-American
10% - Asian-American
 1% - American Indian

INTRODUCTION

Impact in USA

With this increased U.S. heterogeneity has come a resurgence of pride in home country heritages. Until the 1980's, most people living in the U.S. were expected to "assimilate," or adopt the so-called "American" culture evolved from early Northern European settlers. By the time of the 1990 Census, however, 630 separate computer codes had to be created to accommodate all cultural heritages cited in the survey. In today's U.S. society, people seem to want to celebrate their cultural roots and live by those values within an American framework that is being redefined.

The impact of these changes is significant. Whereas in the past we could more or less expect to follow the Anglo-American set of behavioral standards and be effective, this may no longer be the case. In today's multicultural U.S. society, as well as to accommodate global concerns, we must become more informed about other cultures to interact successfully. At stake are our relationships with customers, colleagues in the work place and neighbors in the communities where we live.

This book is dedicated to understanding the nature of diverse cultures, and how we can use this knowledge to communicate more effectively with each other...wherever we may be.

* * *

MULTICULTURAL COMMUNICATION STRATEGIES

"Every action done in company ought to be with some sign of respect to those that are present."

George Washington

CHAPTER 1

THE MEANING OF CULTURE

What does "culture" mean to you? When I ask this question of groups I address, their answers usually boil down to, "the values, traditions and customs of a group of people." Let's look at an excerpt from the New Columbia Encyclopedia's definition, noting also **how** cultures are formed and maintained:

> *"**Culture:** The way of life of a society. The customs, ideas and attitudes shared by a group, which make up its culture, are transmitted from generation to generation by learning processes rather than biological inheritance. Adherence to these customs and attitudes is regulated by systems of rewards and punishments peculiar to each culture."*

Edgar H. Schein, Professor of Management at Massachusetts Institute of Technology (MIT) and mentor to Peter Senge in his development of **The Fifth Discipline** (the learning organization), states simply:

"Culture is the accumulation of past learning."

When we consider the significance of our cultures coming from **learning processes**, rather than biological inheritance, it becomes clear that our cultures have little to do with our genes. Indeed, scientists tell us that, although our behavior may be directed to a certain degree by our genes, the values we follow about how to behave are all learned from the cultural groups to which we are exposed in a lifetime.

Cultural Tree of Life™

An illustration I like to use is that of the *Cultural Tree of Life.™* To create a tree that reflects **your** life, draw your own individual life tree as you read to illustrate for yourself how different cultures have influenced your thinking, and are likely to affect your future attitudes as you go through the passages of time.

At the base of the tree are your roots, i.e. your genes. You were born with these. As the trunk of your tree grows and begins to sprout branches, think of each new twig reaching out for the nourishment of information and, in response, a cultural environment supplies data. You process that information, retaining and rejecting aspects of it in your own individual way. Each new branch, each new leaf has received data from a different cultural group, but has also been influenced by all those which preceded it. This helps to explain why each person on earth is a unique human being, since no one else can duplicate your own set of genes and your own life experiences.

Although we continue to respond to cultures all through life, the cultural values we learn as children, particularly between the ages of one and seven, are the most profound. During these early years we learn concepts from overt teaching as well as via osmosis, or "the unconscious assimilation of the attitudes, values and behavior of those people with whom we have the closest contact" (Webster's Dictionary). These values are modeled and socialized until we reach young adulthood. By the age of twenty it will take a major emotional event to change a value.

Forces of Acculturation

These are some of the forces that can contribute to how the Cultural Tree of Life™ develops:

Family	Neighborhood
Schools	Friends
Gender	Religion
TV/Media	Workplace
Marriage	Parenthood
Profession	Social Status
Relocation	Military

While this is by no means a complete list, it provides a guideline for defining the cultural sources from which we learn (consciously and unconsciously) and the roles these environments can have in our subsequent behavior.

You may have noticed I did not include "ethnicity" in Forces of Acculturation. That is because whatever information we learn about our ethnic backgrounds is learned from others—usually our family and friends. In view of the wide variety of additional influences to which we are exposed in a lifetime, we can see the folly of stereotyping and assuming that because people are of a certain ethnicity they will necessarily follow the behavioral teachings of that culture. Even though that code may be very firm in the home country, many variations from the norm can occur in individuals for a wide variety reasons, particularly in the multicultural USA. Consider these:

Sample Change Factors Causing Differences Within Primary Cultural Groups

Mixtures of Cultural Heritages.

A single cultural heritage is becoming a phenomenon of the past. As the world grows smaller and travel opportunities abound, people meet and mingle, producing families of multiple cultural heritages. And, as we are learning, there are many forms of culture. These mixtures, by definition, produce variety and unpredictability.

Recently I heard a black/Jewish/American Indian woman describing how she would "swing" from culture to culture, depending on circumstances. When she grew up she associated mostly with the African/Americans in her neighborhood. At that time, living in New York, she thought all white women were Jewish (due to the large population of Jews in New York City). Then, in college, she met other American Indians and affiliated with them. Now, as a professional working in a cosmopolitan area, she is interested in exploring **all** her roots.

The concept of "swinging" from culture to culture also applies to generations. A pattern seen frequently in the past is that of the first generation immigrant adhering primarily to the home country culture, the second generation wanting to do everything the "American" way, and the third generation seeing the value of both and combining them into a new culture. In these days of accelerating change we are seeing this transition take place within one generation.

Regional Differences.

As you travel from place to place, you may have noticed how people's overall attitudes change, even between regions in the same country.

A relocated neighbor told me that in Nebraska a handshake means everything and a written contract means nothing. Conversely, while living in New York I learned that a handshake means nothing; eight contracts may have to be signed to consummate a business deal.

An African-American woman in one of my groups talked about her emigration to Detroit from Alabama. Although more job opportunities were available in Detroit, she missed the close sense of community she had in Alabama.

Gender.

Society frequently does not treat boys and girls the same as they grow up, often resulting in dissimilar expectations and images of their roles in life. This phenomenon will be discussed in greater detail in Chapter 3 of this book.

Age.

Since we are most impressionable in childhood, our external environment during those early years contributes to the formation of lasting values. For example, people who grew up during the Depression often remain frugal and debt-free. Those who grew up after World War II, in a relative period of affluence, are more likely to spend money today to make their current lives more pleasant, rather than save it for future contingencies; they may never have known serious economic deprivation. The "generation gaps" we hear about are often due to differences in perceived value, caused by the varying circumstances of people during their childhood years. These problems are exacerbated when younger generations patronize older ones, and vice versa.

Education.

The level of education attained (including cultural education) will have a direct bearing on people's attitudes. The more we learn, the more aware we become that our way may not be the only—or the best—way.

Personal Style.

Our genes, combined with our evironmental learnings, affect how our personalities develop. There are different personal styles within all cultural groups. (See more on this subject in the next chapter.)

Class Status.

In social structures people often find themselves in different social, economic and job rankings, which may even dictate how they should behave and interact with each other. Many languages incorporate class differentiations, such as in forms of address. Therefore, expectations within the classes, as well as society's expectations of the classes, vary. People feel pressure to conform to these expectations, even if they don't agree with them.

* * *

These are but a few of the factors which can cause deviations from cultural norms. Our cultures teach us a set of standards by which we may or may not want to live, sometimes in conflict with continuing pressures to conform to those standards.

Edward C. Stewart has been deemed a "Living Intercultural Legend" by the International Society for Intercultural Education, Training and Research (SIETAR). In his words, "the individual or the group, anyone's past, is in fact unique, so the human condition is one of diversity and not one of uniformity. The function of a culture concept is to organize diversity."

In one of our recent training exercises, people were asked to define for themselves their primary cultural group affiliation, and characteristic strengths of those groups. Their answers illustrate the diversity we see in ourselves. Remember, these are their own definitions of groups and traits listed in *their* priorities:

African	**Hispanic**
Unity	Love of life
Self-determination	Shares emotions
Purpose	Loyalty
Collective responsibility	Humility
Collective economics	Quiet pride
Creativity	Laughter, fun
Respect for family/elders	Family emphasis
Sense of humanity	Strong faith
Respect for spirituality/faith	Relationships-key
Harmony-others/nature	Time relative to people/values
	Hard-working

White Female	**White Male**
Sensitivity	Confidence
Adaptability	Aggressive
Fortitude/determination	Head of family (including finances)
Emotional strength	
Work ethic/doers	Open to change
Conciliatory	Hero
Nurturing/caring	Fix things
Openness/communicative	Leadership/decision makers
Confrontive (a plus)	
Integrity	Male bonding
	Successful

Single Female Parent

Multi-tasked:
- Mother/Father
- Primary Caretaker
- Breadwinner
- Private Life
- Activities
- Community/Church

Well-balanced:
- Work/Play
- Self/Others

Goal-oriented

Responsible
Not Selfish
Organized
Optimistic
Communicator
Diverse
Resilient
Creative
Efficient
Clear self-image

By now it may have occurred to you that *each* of us is "multicultural." In an episode of the popular television series, "Star Trek," the technologically advanced robot character of Dana discovered that within him he had a culture of his own experiences...just like his human counterparts. Therefore, we all have common ground from which to tackle our multicultural communication challenges. Coming up next!

* * *

"The theory of (this book) is that there are no Latinos, only diverse people struggling to remain who they are while becoming someone else. Each of them has a history, which may be forgotten, muddled, misrepresented, misunderstood, but not erased. Every people has its own Eden, and there are no parallel tracks."

Earl Shorris
Latinos: A Biography of the People

CHAPTER 2

Multicultural Communication Model

With all of the cultural influences working on people as they go through life, how are we ever to know the best way to communicate with others? In this chapter we'll look at a simple four-step model, and review specific applications of these concepts through examples and case studies.

Step 1. Approach People As Individuals First.

We've seen in the first chapter how many forces play a part in making each person unique. Therefore, even though we can see that a person appears to have certain ethnic characteristics, we should resist stereotyping and automatically treating people according to their primary culture's customs.

Particularly in America, people often want to be evaluated strictly on their own merits. When I ask people how they would like to be identified, they usually answer "Sam" or "Lynn," not African-American or Asian.

I can relate to that. Having been born and raised in the same Midwestern community, what a thrill it was for me when I moved to New York and, for the first time in my life, was accepted for what I could contribute as a unique individual—not as someone's little sister.

Another example occurred over the holidays when a young Asian sales clerk approached me in a department store. His whole demeanor projected that he was thoroughly westernized. His shirtsleeves were rolled up, he had a contemporary haircut, and wore a big red bow tie. He virtually exuded enthusiasm and energy as he asked me, "How can I help you?" Even though I had learned previously that many Asians prefer a more reserved indirect style, he obviously did not. For me not to have responded in kind would have been a rebuff.

Which brings us to the following principle: we get along best with people when we treat them the way they want to be treated, which is usually a **mirror reflection** of how they act. This is especially true when we first meet them and haven't yet had an opportunity to get to know them.

For instance, when a client greets you at the door with a big smile and firm handshake, try returning the smile and handshake with equal energy, even if your natural style is more subdued. This equalization will get you on the same wave-length, so to speak, to conduct your business compatibly.

Conversely, if *your* style is more out-going, and your client's more reserved, try reining in that enthusiasm to a level more comfortable for your customer, at least at the intial stages. This type of mirroring can help establish rapport and form a solid base to take you to your next communication step.

Inherent in this first step is being aware of your *own* multiculural style, how you are likely to think and act, and proactively controlling your responses to be most effective with the other person...in a sense, to speak their cultural language.

Step 2. Listen, Observe and Clarify.

As you are mirroring the other person's demeanor, put your active listening skills to work.

Everything we do, even when we are immobile, sends a message. Research indicates that only 7 per cent of communication occurs through words in a one-to-one situation. The remaining 38 per cent is through the voice (tone, rate and inflection) and 55 percent through the face and body.

Listen.

Listen for content non-judgmentally; try to be open in evaluating what is being said. Anglo-Americans tend to concentrate on the words primarily, but the *feelings* behind the facts indicate where the real message lies. With more task-oriented indirect people, the signals may be subtle. Is the voice loud, soft, fast, modulated? What clues can you find in the choice of words—is the speaker angry, happy, frustrated, sad?

Observe.

The face is the best source for information. Is it flushed, composed? Is eye contact being avoided? If so, try to determine why (keeping in mind possible cultural reasons, which we explore later.) In Asian cultures, a flaring of the eyes may be the only sign of displeasure.

Is the posture defensive, assertive, combative? Are arms crossed (which could indicate resistance to you or, with more indirect styles, a protective mechanism).

What do the gestures tell you? What emotions are being expressed? Watch for patterns in these body messages, and be alert to changes or discrepancies.

Clarify.

To show the speaker you are listening, and to get more information, ask open-ended questions periodically, such as "Tell me about it," or "Give me an example." Use the mirroring concept when you are in this mode to show the speaker you are empathetic.

Then, to clarify the messages you have received, use "I" statements to paraphrase periodically what you have understood, such as, "So, I understand you perceived an insult from her statement and are not sure what you should do about it." Reflecting what the speaker has said shows you were listening and you care about getting the message accurately. You may even want to incorporate your perception of their feelings about what has been said.

If *you* are in an instructional mode, ask the other person to restate what they have understood; then, if there is confusion, it can be corrected. If the person has an indirect style, emulate that trait by phrasing your questions indirectly.

Be careful, however, about **interrupting**. Morio Itozu, a Japanese consultant born and raised in Tokyo, says (somewhat tongue-in-cheek) that to be fluent in American English you have to develop the skill of interrupting. (See "Going Global? Stifle Yourself!" in our Selected References.)

Allow for silences. Western cultures are often uncomfortable with silence, whereas many other cultures use them for collecting their thoughts, thinking through the issue at hand and creating an impact.

Also, guard against responding automatically, anticipating, daydreaming—or offering advice. Instead, support the speaker in arriving at his/her own conclusions.

Tell the person you appreciate that point of view and, if appropriate to the situation, how complimented you feel about the sharing.

* * *

Sometimes we come to a private conclusion about a person based on our first impressions...and then something happens we don't understand. This is where remembering to consider *all* possible cultural influences comes in handy.

A case in point comes to mind. A young Asian woman in one of my classes had a surface behavior of being totally adapted to American ways. Lydia came bouncing into the session, smiling happily and casually exchanged pleasantries with her fellow employees. She had no trace of an accent, which suggested to me that she had lived in the U.S. for some time. During the class we had a group exercise which required that she work with two of her fellow male workers who had opposite points of view. When the groups reported back to the class, her male colleagues praised her facilitation of bringing them to consensus. As they sang her praises, I noticed that her radiant smile had disappeared and a troubled look had spread across her face. I steered the class away from them and later talked with her in private. I said, "Lydia, what was wrong back there? They were praising you." She looked at me for a moment, then said, "In my culture we are extremely embarassed to be praised in public." So here, even though to all appearances Lydia had adopted most American customs, her cultural heritage still played a role in how she thought, reacted and behaved on a daily basis.

In summary, then, be on the lookout for a unique *blending* of cultural values.

* * *

The first two steps of this communicaton model concentrate on how you should behave during an encounter. The third relies on your having done your homework **before** the encounter, so you can draw on that knowledge to interpret the other person's behavior accurately.

Step 3. Consider Cultural Heritages.

Cultural values are based on perceptions and beliefs about concepts. Communication challenges occur most often when these perceptions and beliefs differ. Let's review some key concepts in the development of cultural heritages and how people think—and feel—in relation to them.

Male Dominance.

Since the beginning of recorded history, most cultures have been dominated by men who, for the most part, held the world's power. The need to survive in a hostile world and maintain order drove many of these concepts. Although the balance of gender influence is changing, the male point of view has had the most significant role in shaping all the following historical cultural traditions. It should also be noted that today the values of many men are changing, too, adding to the multicultural complexity of individuals (See Chapter 1).

Individualism vs. Group Orientation.

Most cultural differences throughout the world stem from these two perspectives. Once you digest the implications of these concepts, the applications are infinite.

In 1835 Alexis de Tocqueville, French author of the classic book **Democracy in America**, coined the term "individualism" to describe the American character, as a result of his travels through the U.S. The historical

Anglo-American culture is based on the freedom of individuals to develop themselves to their fullest potential. The values of the dominant culture are by definition the values of the entrepreneur, the reasons why many immigrants come to America: freedom to achieve one's "personal best" and prosper. America was designed to be a democracy where each person's point of view counts.

Typical acculturation begins with America's traditional classroom seating arrangements, teaching procedures and grading systems, where competition is encouraged among students to be the "first with the correct answer," write the "best" essay and, generally, be the "winner."

Compare this perspective to that of most other world cultures which value the group over the individual. In Japanese schools, for example, the classroom is arranged with circular seating. When the teacher asks a question, students within each group confer with each other, reach a consensus, and then raise their hands in unison with their joint answer. Skills at facilitating group decisions are learned.

Translated into the working environment, the Anglo-American approach often encourages individual achievement through competition with one another for financial incentives and promotions, a process which has been credited with much of America's success. (If not managed appropriately, however, it can result in a lack of cooperation and absence of true team spirit in the workplace.) The social group orientation, on the other hand, has been credited with the recent success of many Asian countries. In Japan, for example, it has helped them build effective teams and work together for the common good of the company and the country. (However, final decisions are likely to be delayed until there is group consensus, and individual interests are usually not considered.) Perhaps the best approach is a customized blend of the two approaches to best meet the situation.

Aspiring to excellence is present in all cultures. The difference lies in who gets the credit—the individual or the group. In America individual accomplishment reflects back primarily to the person who made the achievement. In group-oriented cultures, the glory is shared by the family, company and/or country.

Group-oriented people want to "fit in," to feel that they belong and are accepted, not singled out. This may show up in surprising ways. I had an engagement at a manufacturing plant in Texas where the CEO was East Indian. He had been living in the U.S. for the past 20 years. I happened to run into him on my way into the plant that morning and, because I knew a more formal protocol was observed in India, I asked him how he would like me to address him in front of the class. He paused, looked at me somewhat strangely, then said his first name. I thanked him and wondered privately about his reaction. Later in the day, during a break, he approached me. He said, "Judith, I know you care about this subject, so I want to share something with you. When you asked me about my name, I felt singled out." What is the message here? For him, the primary group he wanted to be associated with—at least in this setting—was his company, his employees. He just wanted to be treated like "one of the guys."

Relationships are key with group-oriented people. Trust comes slowly but, once earned, bonds of loyalty ensue. Therefore, to violate that relationship is to violate that trust, and severe repercussions may result. High relationship cultures value subjective factors like loyalty, process and perseverance and can be insulted by "objective" measurements and reward systems. Many blacks, American Indians, Hispanics and women share these values.

Individualism also stems from a basic distrust of tradition. The people who founded the country were fleeing from oppressive institutions. They wanted freedom to live their lives without external restrictions. That attitude of challenging existing authority and tradition continues to permeate American society today. Americans are always looking for ways to improve the present.

An aspect of the individualistic outlook is to prize the imagination and creativity of each person. American ingenuity has been responsible for much of the nation's success. Brainstorming, a popular American method of gleaning ideas from groups, requires that the individual offer ideas for group consideration as they occur, without evaluation or judgment. Such offerings require courage, sometimes, because the ideas may at first appear to be foolish, particularly in the eyes of others. As a result, some cultural groups (such as Asians, American Indians and some Hispanics) may be reluctant to join into the process, fearing to lose face in the eyes of the group members. This also explains their reluctance to respond negatively when asked questions; to them such a response would be construed as being rude and disrespectful. People who honor others before themselves need to be encouraged to excel as individuals and to be assured that they will not be ridiculed for their views.

Self-reliance is considered a virtue by many Americans. A popular saying of early Anglican settlers was, "The Lord helps those who help themselves." Although many cultures encourage self-development, it is usually toward the advancement of the common good rather than for self-aggrandizement. In America, land of the entrepreneur, "self-made" success stories are often considered to be the highest accolade a person could receive. In societies where "the nail that sticks out gets hammered down," such a notion is tantamount to blasphemy.

A final note regarding the concept of individuality vs. group orientation. Traditionally strong group societies such as Japan's are beginning to see more value in developing individuality. Japan's Ministry of Education opened a new school in April of 1995 with "the mission of being a pioneering school to develop individuality." This still controversial school was in response to the criticism of many corporate leaders and critics who believe the current educational system fails to develop the work force Japan will need in the 21st Century.

Conversely, there are also applications of group orientation *within* the individualistic American culture, such as identifying strongly with one's employer and affiliating with organizations whose causes we admire. According to W. Hampton Sides, at heart we are joiners:

> "Modern America is a country of subcultures, a place where people's identities are shaped to a peculiar extent

by the private enthusiasms which they may pursue with kindred spirits within an identifiable microcosm."

As the saying goes, achieving the right balance is the key.

Religion.

In many group-oriented cultures, religious views permeate every aspect of life, including the language, everyday behavior, work and politics. The concept of separating church and state is relatively rare throughout the world.

At the risk of over-simplification, here are a few core concepts of religions and life philosophies most followed throughout the world. All of these are represented in the U.S.

Buddhism values harmony and moderation. "A religion of eastern and central Asia growing out of the teaching of Gautama Buddha that suffering is inherent in life and that one can be liberated from it by mental and moral self-purification" (Webster's Dictionary). To maintain harmony, confrontation will be avoided. In Zen Buddhist sects, the master's role is to raise puzzling questions, and the students must find their own answers.

Christianity, the religion derived from Jesus Christ, is based on the Bible as sacred scripture, and is professed by Eastern, Roman Catholic and Protestant bodies. Followers believe that Jesus Christ was and is the Son of God. Christianity teaches conformity with the ethics of generosity and concern for others, and to follow the teachings of Jesus Christ and his disciples. It is the majority religion in the U.S.

Confucianism is more of an approach to life, relating to the Chinese philosopher Confucius' central emphasis on the practice and cultivation of the cardinal virtues of filial piety, kindness, righteousness, propriety, intelligence and faithfulness. These have historically formed the basis of much of Chinese ethics, education, statecraft and religion.

Hinduism is the dominant religion of India, emphasizing dharma (conformity to one's duty to divine law and nature) with its resulting ritual and social observances and often mystical contemplation and ascetic practices.

Islam, the religious faith of Muslims, includes the belief in Allah as the sole deity and in Muhammad as his prophet. "Islam" also refers to the civilization erected upon Islamic faith, as well as the group of modern nations in which Islam is the dominant religion, located in the Middle East, Africa, Asia and elsewhere.

Judaism is a religion developed among the ancient Hebrews. It is characterized by belief in one transcendent God who has revealed himself to Abraham, Moses and the Hebrew prophets, and by a religious life in accordance with Scriptures and rabbinic traditions. It also refers to the cultural, social and religious beliefs and practices of the Jewish people.

Kwanzaa, while not a religion, epitomizes the moral values of many African-Americans. At year-end African-Americans observe this seven-day holiday, bridging cultural gaps and downplaying commercialism. These values are celebrated: unity, self-determination, collective work and responsibility, cooperative economics, purpose, creativity and faith.

Authority/Hierarchy.

Group-oriented cultures tend to respect authority within a hierarchical framework. Modesty is deemed appropriate; the boss will know if you are doing a good job and will reward you appropriately. In deference to authority, Asians and Hispanics will wait for the boss to initiate. If the boss is Anglo-American, he/she is likely to be waiting for the *subordinates* to initiate.

Geert Hofstede, renowned interculturalist, refers to what he calls "power distance: the extent the less powerful members of organizations and institutions accept unequal power distribution. Power distance is partially measured by the degree of comfort subordinates feel in contradicting or negotiating with superiors." In his studies, Asian countries measured high in respecting power distance, meaning the less powerful were reluctant to challenge those in power, while Western industrialized countries measured on the lower end of this dimension, illustrating their inclination to challenge existing authority.

In another cultural example, Latinos may not speak openly in a meeting because they do not want to appear to take away the "seat of honor" from the person presiding over the meeting.

Respect for authority is expressed through speech and behavior. In working with a financial organization in New York, a Chinese-American female controller was trying to improve her communication techniques. In her mind her position of authority required that she behave in a somewhat dictatorial manner in order to be respected by subordinates. She had been informed by her boss, however, that she needed to communicate better with her employees, that she tended to "talk down" to them. After learning about the importance of two-way communication, she established opportunites for that purpose. However, she still had not understood that she needed to act on the information she learned from them. Yes, she listened to her people, but then she went right ahead and did what she had planned to do all along. Change sometimes comes slowly.

An offshoot of respect for authority is the concept of "**choice**," which may be new to recently-arrived immigrants. To appreciate what this may mean to people, think of the first time you realized that you—and you alone—were **responsible** for the choices you made. It may have been when you were a child; for some immigrants they are only now facing that reality. It's much easier when someone else has the responsibility to choose. If the choice turns out to be a bad one, it's "their fault."

Filial Piety.

Another aspect of respecting authority is that of filial piety, respect for the elderly and the extended family. In most Asian cultures there is a strong sense of obligation to make certain older members of the family are taken care of and honored, embracing Confucianism.

This piety is even expressed in the language used.

Language.

Cultures valuing hierarchy and formality are reserved in their forms of address. I recently worked with a group of African-Americans who referred to each other as "Miss," "Mrs." or "Mr.," never by their first names. Anglo-Americans, who like to create an atmosphere of informality as soon as possible, frequently go to first names immediately and, to get even more informal, create nicknames from them. For example, it is not uncommon when being introduced to someone in America as Robert Jones to return the introduction with, "Hi, Bob, glad to meet you." While this is intended to be "friendly," it may not be received that way. A safe rule to follow is call a person by the name he or she uses until given permission by that person to use a more familiar term.

Protocol regarding familiarity in addressing people is built into many languages, and people of other cultures may be offended by American eagerness to establish immediate rapport. Trust comes only with time among group-oriented relationships, and must be earned. Blacks don't like being asked a lot of personal questions.

The English language is a tool to be used; the Japanese language is part of the experience to be lived. In a 1993 study by **Child Development**, researchers found that when interacting with their infants, Japanese mothers foster mutual dependence. From the mother's speech, the infant begins to acquire not only the rules of the language, but also the norms of the culture. American mothers worked toward fostering independence in their infants.

The Chinese compose their writings in a circular way; to start with the main message is abrupt, rude. For example, a student writer may begin an essay by using an oblique metaphor, such as, "the cherry blossoms bloom in a lovely mist," but her Anglo-American teacher may be impatient for her to make the point more directly.

Self.

In some hierarchical group-oriented cultures there is no concept of "self" as Americans understand it. One exists only in relation to others. A Korean husband refers to "our" wife, as his spouse belongs to the whole family. Sons are referred to as the "elder" or "younger" brother. The father/son relationship is paramount in the family unit. There is no word for "privacy" in the Japanese language. In China the individual has little significance; the family comes first, and everything one does reflects on one's ancestors.

This can be offsetting to managers who are trying to empower their workforces if the employees are unaccustomed to thinking of themselves in such powerful roles. A Minneapolis manufacturer has been coping with this syndrome in managing a group of Hmong refugees.

In a Cuban American household, the first generation father complains to his American-raised children when they close the doors of their rooms for privacy. He feels this is a mark of their assimilation into the American culture, away from adherence to the family and toward independence.

With many blacks, Hispanics, Asians and white women, there is a sense of shame and embarassment in self-promotion. Anglo-American males, on the other hand, often take the view, "If you've got it, flaunt it."

In the American-style performance appraisal process it is unlikely that an Asian, Hispanic, American Indian, some blacks and even some Anglo-American women will offer self-praise for their past peformance; it is assumed that the authority figure will already know their level of performance and will make the appropriate evaluation. For them, modesty is virtuous. In addition, their respect for authority figures may impede their inclination to speak on behalf of themselves. If appraisers do not understand this assumption and, consequently, appraise the individual as lacking self-confidence, they can severely devalue the true contributions of the person, as well as create a demoralizing work environment. Understanding the values of the individual being reviewed are critical to accurate assessment.

On the other hand, many western North Europeans who have emigrated to the United States in recent years had become accustomed in their homeland to a work setting where the views of employees carry almost as much weight with management as those of the supervisors. If the appraiser happens to have a directorial style of management, he or she may be dismayed by the candor of the employee. Adjustments to this opposite level of honesty and self-worth may be needed by the supervisor.

Individualists often have a high task orientation related to action. In America, a common question when meeting a new person is, "What do you do?," implying that one's work-related activity defines the most significant aspect of an individual's identity. Most group cultures, where one's primary identity is linked to one's ancestry, may consider such a question to be odd or even rude, depending upon how accepting the person is of American ways.

Saving Face (Avoiding Shame).

More than anything else, the Japanese fear mistakes and rejections. Mistakes to them show lack of preparation, competence and dedication. Failures bring shame not only to the individual, but to the group as well. Similarly, Japanese dread rejection. Rejection indicates failure to have adequately prepared and insincerity in work efforts.

There was a best-selling book in Japan designed for American businessmen titled, **Never Take "Yes" For An Answer.** In many Asian, as well as Hispanic and American Indian societies, it is rude to answer a question with "no." Indeed, in the Japanese language, there are 16 different meanings for the word "yes." It can mean anything from "Yes, I will do my best," to "Yes, I don't want to embarrass you," to "Yes, I don't want to bring shame on my family by admitting an error," to "Yes, we will consider it."

A result of this concept can be that people will not ask for help, or ask questions if they do not understand; to do so would be shameful in their eyes. So it is up to us to follow the clarification rule (Step 2 of the Communication Model) and, indirectly, be sure the situation is understood correctly.

For Mexicans, personal dignity is important from the moment of birth to the moment of death. Pride is a significant aspect of the Mexican culture.

When interacting with people who value these concepts, refer to your personal relationship with them and express your personal need for their cooperation in order to save face.

Eye Contact.

In Arab and American cultures, eye contact is a sign of sincerity, while in Japan it can be seen as potentially threatening and is usually avoided.

In many Anglo-American families, children are taught that direct eye contact connotes honesty, forthrightness and strength of character. A schoolteacher colleague reported recently that, when she tried to teach this definition to her students, a black child told her that his mother reprimanded him if he looked her directly; to her it was a sign of defiance and disrespect. This latter view is shared by many blacks (particularly those raised in southern states), Asians, American Indians and some Hispanics.

Different Asian cultures may have conflict with each other; Filipino's, Koreans and Vietnamese feel that direct eye contact with each other can be dangerous.

If you tend to look at people directly, and they don't look at you, guard against making assumptions about them. After a speaking engagement in Milwaukee a woman approached me with this story. They had just interviewed an American Indian for a job opening they had. He was highly-qualified in every respect, but he wouldn't look any of the interviewers in the eye. They decided not to hire him based solely on his lack of eye contact; they feared he was hiding something. They did not realize that this was his way of showing respect.

Emotional Expression.

The Anglo-American task orientation tends to focus on "getting the job done" over the personal concerns of the people who are doing the job. Indeed, the Anglo-American norm is often distrustful of emotions, assuming that emotions interfere with efficiency. This attitude is largely derived from the Northern European heritage and is still shared today with those cultures.

Asians, too, often follow the Confucian view that one should contain one's emotions, remaining calm and controlled—particularly in public.

On the other hand, the issue of "feelings," or approaching situations in a caring manner, is important to many African-Americans, Hispanics and some women.

These opposing views can lead to misunderstandings, especially when mixed heritages are involved.

A multicultural situation was reported recently by the United Feature Syndicate. A black Asian woman, whose parents were from Sri Lanka, was perceived as "acting white" or "stuck up" because she did not automatically speak to every African-American she encountered in her American workplace, whether she knew them or not. She explained that by nature she was rather reserved and had been taught that it was impolite to speak to strangers unless addressed. In addition, she enjoyed being alone with her thoughts (perhaps the Hindu influence of her homeland). Although her friends and Anglo-Americans accepted her behavior, the black community at large thought she was quite rude.

A strategy for her to consider is the "mirroring" concept discussed earlier to be effective in her working environment; a little flexibility goes a long way. On the other hand, the black community in the above situation might try empathizing and follow the example of an African-American flight supervisor who wanted to comfort Asian families whose loved ones had been killed in a plane crash. In her words, "I wanted to put my arms around them and hug them, but sensed I couldn't. They needed to express their feelings privately. It would have been an invasion of their family grieving."

In classroom debates at the University of Illinois Professor Thomas Kochman discovered that blacks feel the validity of an argument increases with the degree of emotion invested in presenting it. Whites, on the other hand, reacted just the opposite—the more emotion used in debating a point, the less credence they attached to the point being made. In other examples he says, blacks value a chance to learn from "spilling the milk." Asians prefer to learn before any milk is spilled.

The visual style of many blacks (particularly men) is to act deliberately, studying visual cues. When listening, they may not respond with occasional "Uh-Huh's" or even look at the speaker. This can be disconcerting for people who expect certain conversational noise and periodic acknowledgment that the listener is in fact listening. Taking offense can result.

Blacks are often frustrated by the fact that Anglo-Americans and Asians don't want to talk about inflammatory subjects. They may view silence as a sign of hostility. Anglo-Americans tend to assume that if a topic is "hot," there is no potential for further discussion.

Blacks, on the other hand, may believe the opposite and vigorously pursue such a discourse. Passionate statements are often perceived by whites as "potentially violent," whereas blacks consider them to be "earnest representation." To blacks, withdrawal from a discussion signals indifference. Black males may feel "disrespected."

The absence of personal involvement and lack of consideration regarding how people are emotionally affected by the job can result in frustration and anger, interfering with the goals of all concerned. The ultimate task objectives on both sides are the same, but the parties involved differ on **how** to approach accomplishing the task. This is why group-oriented people may show loyalty to their friends and family units over the task to be accomplished for the organization; they believe that the employer is not committed to their best interests, as they believe their close personal group members are.

Smiling.

Smiling is interpreted differently among cultures. Anglo-Americans intend to convey friendliness and acceptance, but may consider excessive smiling to be a sign of weakness. Within the over 60 Asian countries, smiling can be interpreted in several ways, such as friendliness, concealing embarrassment or flirtation (particularly by women). It may be reserved for only close relationships as a sign of intimacy and, therefore, withheld in public situations.

A Russian immigrant was advised to be serious in a job interview. He didn't get the job because they thought he was privately snickering. Lessons here include: be yourself and be aware that how others behave may not be a true reflection of their normal behavior, particularly if they are not on their "home turf."

Touching.

Highly expressive relationship-oriented cultures, such as the Hispanic and African-American, usually feel touching is a natural part of life. However, both have a sense of formality and hierarchy in their group affiliation and may consider touching without permission to be offensive.

Cultures approving a more indirect style, including some Anglo-Americans and Asians, view touching as inappropriate, expressing warmth in other ways. For them, a middle-of-the road approach to life is best, between extremes.

Blacks have become angry with Asian merchants in their neighborhoods because the store owners will avoid touching customers when giving change in a financial transaction. The blacks take personal offense, whereas the Asians are merely following a behavioral style they observe even with friends, out of respect.

It should be noted, however, that touching is also a matter of personal style, and those inclinations vary across cultures.

Negotiating.

Expressive group-oriented cultures often enjoy negotiating. East Indians, Mexicans, and Middle Easterners like the gamesmanship and interpersonal exchange. This is difficult for people used to more formal protocol, where decisions are finite and prices firm. Questioning a price may even be perceived as an insult. Here again, flexibility is the key, making maximum use of Steps 1 and 2 of this communication model.

Time.

Time is specific; time is money in America. One of the first things visitors to the U.S. notice is clocks on every street corner. Time is relative in most other more group-oriented cultures, relative to relationships and long-term interests. A Latino attorney associate of mine explained that if he were on the way to a meeting and ran into an old friend, he would probably be late for the meeting. To him (and to most Latinos) the relationship would take priority.

Asian societies view time as a continuum, an ongoing flowing river, not a commodity to be lost. Mae Jemison, first African-American female astronaut, says, "If I've learned one thing in life, it is don't push the river. It flows by itself."

Space.

People's sense of personal space varies according to their acculturation. It is a matter of hierarchy (acknowledging authority), conditioning (people from densely-crowded cities stand closer to others than those from sparsely-populated farm areas) and beliefs (Middle-Easterners stand very close to one another). People can feel intimidated or offended if their personal space is invaded without permission; it is a cause for some sexual harassment complaints.

Reasoning.

Group-oriented cultures tend to be non-linear in their reasoning, whereas individualists, in their quest to achieve goals in the short-term, more linear. Edward T. Hall, noted interculturalist, has identifed these tendencies as "High Context" and "Low Context." High context people take into account a variety of related factors in solving a problem, whereas low context people consider the more immediate short-term elements. For example, if a machine broke down, the low context person would focus on what was needed to get it running again. A high context person would not only consider these elements, but also what it would cost in terms of labor, down-time and out-of-pocket expense, what it would cost to buy a new one, would these alternatives be cost-effective in the current production schedule, how would a change affect the workers, and should an alternative process be developed to accomplish what the machine did—or, focusing on the forest vs. the tree.

Many group-oriented cultures, particularly Asians and Middle Easterners, have a tolerance for ambiguity that is not shared by low context peoples who want finite answers immediately. Socrates taught that all the answers in the universe lie within us; all we have to do is recognize them. That recognition process can be excruciatingly long for those impatient for tangible results.

Humor.

The expression of humor is related to emotions and respect for authority. If formal hierarchy is valued, humor—particularly in public—can be viewed as frivolous. Informal cultures often use humor to create rapport.

American humor, in accordance with the basic cultural premise of challenging tradition, attacks so-called "sacred cows." Freedom of expression is one of the most prized assets of the culture. At times it seems the more insulting it is, the more people laugh.

More formal cultures, however, may not find such efforts humorous and, even more, offensive. An understanding of your audience is crucial here to accomplish your objective.

Self-deprecatory humor is usually considered acceptable in hierarchical cultures, and can create a bonding between you and your listener. Humorous remarks directed at any culture but your own are risky.

Work and Family.

Family is the most important entity in most group-oriented cultures. It takes priority over everything else. And you always take care of the family.

If an employee requests time off because of a family matter, the manager would be well-advised to pay attention to the individual's cultural heritage. If family takes first priority for the person, an effective strategy could be to show understanding and grant the request. A relationship built upon mutual respect can provide long-term benefits, such as reciprocity when the going gets tough.

Case study: An Asian Indian was requested by his supervisor to come in over a weekend to put in overtime on a critical project. The employee had already made plans to participate in a family religious ceremony. Through negotiation they agreed that the employee would complete the ceremony, then come into the plant afterwards. By appreciating each other's dilemmas, they were able to derive a solution that met each other's needs and strengthened their relationship.

* * *

Keep in mind the above are **historical** values and may not be held by the people you meet. Remember, we are all multicultural and living in a constantly changing world. Use Step 1 (Approach People as Individuals First) and Step 2 (Listen, Observe and Clarify) to help you determine what cultural heritages may be influencing each encounter.

* * *

THE ROLE OF PERSONAL STYLES

Interpersonal preferences can be a matter of personal style, not just culture. Personal styles vary across all cultures. Good communication begins with self-awareness.

As far back as Greek mythology there are references to the thesis that all humans have four different styles or personality types. An early scientific documentation occurred in 450 B.C. when the physician Hippocrates wrote of four basic temperaments in people.

More recently, beginning with Carl Jung's work in the 1920's, behavioral scientists have refined these concepts through extensive research. Now many tools exist on the market to help people understand themselves, and others, more clearly.

Research to date indicates each of us has a unique *combination* of these four styles, with one or two preferred in most situations. Self-assessment instruments reveal our own preferences, explain those of others, and give us the option to manage our own behavior when interacting with others. If managed appropriately, a more constructive social environment can result. An examination of the four basic styles in conjunction with historical cultural norms can help us see where correlations lie.

First, a caveat. People do not always feel comfortable with the cultural norm of their primary group. In fact, there may well be conflict between the personal style of an individual and the cultural norm to which he or she feels duty-bound to conform. This becomes clear when we remember that researchers have concluded our personal style preferences are a result of our genes combined with our environment, particularly during our formative years. As societies evolve, and the individual rights of both genders are valued by the culture, changes in norms are also evolving. For now, however, we will review personal styles in the context of

historical ethnic norms, which still dominate most societies.

Individualistic Styles.

The first two personal styles correlate with North American and Northern European cultures. They are primarily task-oriented, focusing on data to provide the answers to living well. Progress is measured in tangibles. Goals are action-oriented and geared to produce short-term material profits. The societies are structured to honor individuals who succeed financially. The driving force of the culture is work which, therefore, is the usual context in which a person is honored; this explains why self-esteem is often linked to one's position in the workplace. Emotions are suspect and considered inappropriate in most social and work settings.

Characteristics of these styles are:

> **Style 1.** Highly individualistic, assertive, directive, dominating, results-oriented, independent, strong-willed, competitive, formal, quick decision makers, impatient, time-conscious, authoritative, problem-solving, control-seeking, well-organized.

> **Style 2.** Highly analytical, indirect, nonemotional, perfectionistic, self-directed, have a long attention span, objective, serious, persistent, structured, diplomatic, formal, time-disciplined, follow directions well, problem-solving, self-contained, and have a high need to be recognized for

their individual performance. Edward T. Hall might also call these "low context," in that they prefer to see matters in absolutes, such as "black or white" with no grey areas, taking matters at face value.

Group Styles.

The third and fourth personal styles correlate more closely with group-oriented societies, honoring the relationships of their cultural group before that of an "outgroup," such as company or country. Family and community ties are strong; feelings and emotions are valued and encouraged to be expressed; religious and spiritual beliefs are deep. Referring again to Hall's definitions, these styles would be "high context," in that behavior is viewed in a complex way. They look beyond the obvious to note nuances in meaning, nonverbal communication cues and the status of others in context.

Characteristics of these styles are:

Style 3. Indirect, highly affiliative, team-oriented, systematic, steady, quiet, patient, loyal, dependable, informal, servicing, predictable, sharing, like staying in one place, slow decision-makers, respectful, good listeners.

Style 4. Assertive, spontaneous, talkative, gregarious, leading, fast-paced, stimulating, creative, risk-taking, enthusiastic, friendly, playful, like the spotlight, thrive on dynamics of relationships, unstructured, open and direct.

You may have already considered that there are obvious cultural groups which tend to bridge more than one style (Styles 2 and 3, for instance, apply to most Japanese). As we mentioned earlier, individuals have some elements of all four styles, to varying degrees. Combined with our individual life experiences (remember the Cultural Tree of Life™), it becomes even more crucial to use Steps 1 and 2 of the Communication Model when evaluating the personal styles of people, and then respond with how **they** want to be treated, regardless of the cultural context in which you meet.

When we use these concepts, we are empowered to **manage our own** style preferences to maximum development and effectiveness with others.

Step 4. Develop Dialogues & Relationships.

The final step in this communication model is to develop ongoing dialogues and fruitful relationships with people of all cultures. Getting to know individual people is one of the best ways possible to really understand each other. Here are some pointers to get started:

When interacting with someone for whom English is a second language, remember these suggestions:

MULTICULTURAL COMMUNICATION MODEL

- Speak slowly and distinctly, pausing after each main point if a translator is being used. Use simple sentences.

- Avoid using slang, jargon, colloquialisms or sports metaphors—or talking baby talk.

- Use word pictures and illustrations to clarify your points.

- If the person does not seem to understand, don't talk louder or "down" to them, as you would to a child. (It seems to be a natural reaction to do this.) Instead, try rephrasing what you said, with the attitude of "I'm sorry, I did not make myself clear."

- If you do not understand, be polite and say that you are having a little difficulty in understanding them and request that they repeat.

- Have a language aid nearby to help you with immediate translations.

- Be aware of your words, gestures and their meanings.

In your everyday dealings, remember these points:

- An individualistic person will probably want to be very direct and open with you; a group-oriented person more indirect and non-revealing until trust is established.

- For those who believe in formal hierarchy and/or are highly group-oriented, you may want to have a trusted intermediary introduce you, someone both of you trust. That person may need to be present until the third party is comfortable with you. Several meetings may be necessary before you can conduct business.

- Look for clues to their cultural orientation and personal style, using Steps 1 and 2 of the Communication Model. Respond according to their needs.

- Select a topic of conversation of mutual interest which sets you on equal footing, which may be unrelated to business—such as the weather or kids. Build on similarities—we all have a lot in common. Beware of getting too personal too soon, however.

- Treat people with respect. Everyone on this planet wants their human dignity acknowledged.

- Talk in a normal tone of voice, as a peer vs. a boss or subordinate.

- Be positive and good-humored in your demeanor and speech. If you have a question, ask it pleasantly and try to maintain a positive attitude as you continue the conversation, even if you have a complaint. You may be surprised at the pleasant outcome.

MULTICULTURAL COMMUNICATION MODEL

- Guard against taking offense at something that is said or done; it may have been innocent. Consider the possible cultural reason or intent. Be non-judgmental.

- Use "I" statements when you speak, demonstrating that you take responsibility for what you are thinking and feeling. This takes the onus off them and helps to clarify your position. For example, you could say, "I perceive that you are angry about...Am I correct?" rather than saying "You are angry."

- Elicit feedback. Ask, don't assume. Check out your assumptions and perceptions. Communication is a two-way dialogue. Empathize.

- Keep the dialogue going—maintain the relationship.

Many companies today are creating employee discussion groups that meet regularly to air out matters of dissension, bridge differences, and come to mutual resolution. In some, managers are included. In all, management receives feedback.

* * *

For more information on cultures in home countries see our chapter on International Philosophies and Protocol.

Never Met A Man I Didn't Like*

Try the shoes on that are his,
Feel what makes him what he is,
What it's like inside his skin,
Livin' in the skin he's in,
Just like me, a lump of sod,
There but for the grace of God,
That is the philosophy,
Of this part-time Cherokee.

Never met a man I didn't like.

*Based on the words of Will Rogers
Excerpt from* **The Will Rogers Follies**

---

*NEVER MET A MAN I DIDN'T LIKE, music by Cy Coleman, Lyrics by Betty Comden and Adolph Green
©1991 Notable Music Co., Inc. and Betdolph Music Company
All Rights administered by WB Music Corp.
All Rights Reserved   Used by Permission
WARNER BROS. PUBLICATIONS U.S. INC., Miami, FL. 33014

CHAPTER 3

THE CULTURES OF GENDER

A fiftyish white man approached me during break at a workshop we were giving. I could tell he was having trouble finding the right words, but he wanted to talk. He said, "You know, I thnk it's good that women are taking on more responsibility in the work force, and I want to work with them effectively, but I'm not sure what to say to them. I'm a man of action, not words. In a way it's like everything you've been taught your whole life has just changed almost overnight. Where is all this heading?" I could tell this was just the tip of an iceberg of concerns, and I wondered how many other men felt the same way.

Garrison Keillor summed up the situation this way in his 1993 **The Book of Guys**:

> "Guys are in trouble these days. Years ago, manhood was an opportunity for achievement and now it is a problem to be overcome. Guys who once might have painted the ceiling of the Sistine Chapel or composed **Don Giovanni** are now just trying to be Mr. O.K. All-Rite, the man who can bake a cherry pie, converse easily

51

about intimate things, cry, be vulnerable, be passionate in a skillful way, and yet also be the guy who lifts them bales and totes that barge."

These sentiments are the result of some dramatic changes in the role of women in America. Ever since the 19th amendment was passed in 1920 giving women the right to vote, women have been gradually gaining a more viable place in society. Today almost 60 percent of the female population works (as of a 1994 U.S. Bureau of Labor Statistics study) and, according to a May 22, 1995, article in **Newsweek**, earn about as much as men in nearly half of American households.

Men have reacted in a variety of ways. While they like wives' earnings, they are mixed on career goals. University of Michigan researchers found in a May 1995 survey that husbands found it easier to accept their wives' decision to work in order to provide for their families, than when the women were seeking status and personal satisfaction through a career.

In reaction to this change in their age-old roles, man are bonding together in various "men's movements," both within and outside of the work force.

An organization called the Promise Keepers attracted huge male audiences (e.g, 64,000 in Chicago, 72,500 in Los Angeles and 67,000 in Denver) in twelve conferences nationwide during 1995. Its premise is: Christian men make promises to take responsibility, love and respect their wives, spend more time with their families, make and keep commitments, and *really* open up with other men. (Critics of the movement say the group also promotes the dominance of men and the submission of women, even if it is supposed to be in a loving environment.)

This premise echoes the movement started by Robert Bly (see **Iron John** in our References section) and others in the 1980's to help men open up emotionally with each other (especially their fathers) through analogies to their warrior ancestors. And, in the process, celebrate their manhood.

In the work force men are also "flocking together." In many companies, support groups for men only are being formed to help them respond to the threat of what many consider to be their inherent right to rule. Participants represent all racial and cultural groups, as well as all position levels within the organization. At DuPont, for example, the premise behind their Men's Forum is:

> "Until a man faces his own work regarding race, gender and sexual orientation, he is stuck in repeating traditional patterns of dominance. These patterns restrict a man's identity and the depth of his relationships. Growing consciousness brings each man possibilities for enriching his life."

This forum is intended to produce a framework for understanding self and exploring one's full potentialities, as well as provide tools to deal with a changing work force.

How do women feel about their new global roles? A July 26, 1995, feature in **The Wall Street Journal** reports, "Around the world, women are remaking companies, society and themselves. But in each country, women have achieved different things, fought different battles—and made different sacrifices." Representative countries are capsulized as:

> **"Japan:** She is free, yet she's alone in her world."
>
> **"Mexico:** For a woman it takes perhaps triple the effort to succeed in the land of *machismo*."
>
> **"Sweden:** Laws help Mom, but they hurt her career."
>
> **"United States:** Success at a huge personal cost."

The changing roles of men and women in business and society have put new pressures on the age-old challenge of gender compatibility. To define effective strategies for coping with these new circumstances, we need to examine the foundations of historic male/female relationships.

Let's start with the brain. **Time** reported July 17, 1995, that "gender may bend your thinking." Based on studies of a growing number of scientists, evidence is mounting that men and women may think in subtly distinctive ways. To summarize: "Both sides of a woman's brain are used in processing language; a man's mind is more compartmentalized." (To refer back to Edward T. Hall's concepts, one might say that men tend to be more Low Context in their thinking patterns, and women, more High Context.) A similar article in **Newsweek**, March 27, 1995, reported further that sensitivity training also plays a role in brain development. "If the first tantalizing findings (of new techniques for brain imaging) are any clue, the research will show that our identities as men and women are creations of both nature and nurture."

Which brings us to the power of acculturation. My black female colleagues tell me that everyone in the African-American community knows, "We raise our daughters, and love our sons."

The custom of favoring the male of the species is not limited to blacks. In 1990 the American Association of University Women conducted a ground-breaking poll across cultures which highlighted how many girls' self-esteem gradually plummets as they grow up—in spite of women's advances in society and, in some cases, their own families. Although girls begin first grade with the same levels of skill and ambitions as boys, by the time they reach high school, all too often, "their doubts have crowded out their dreams."

Journalist Peggy Orenstein humanizes the study's statistics in her book, **SchoolGirls**, wherein she explores the influences of home, school and society on how girls and boys are raised to think about themselves. These are some of her observations, based on a year spent with eighth graders at two California schools (one affluent, one lower socio-economic), as well as interviews with parents and teachers:

> Boys want to get ahead.
> Girls want to get along.

Boys see themselves as better than girls.
Girls see themselves as equal to boys.

Boys snap their fingers to get attention, and are rewarded for this behavior by the teacher.
Girls keep their hands up till called on.

Girls are taught overtly to fulfill their potential, but learn other negative messages subliminally.

Girls' self-esteem is tied strongly into how they look—their appearance.

Middle-class white girls often become anorexic. Black urban girls like bigness, equating it with survival and power. Their strategy to succeed is to stay away from boys.

Latina girls still suffer from *machismo* stereotyping by family and the educational system. They are vulnerable to gangs, particularly in the inner city.

How do these early acculturations, as well as male/female brain tendencies, manifest themselves in adults...particularly in the multicultural work force?

Deborah Tannen, a linguistics professor at Georgetown University, has published several studies on gender communication research. She and other researchers have generally concurred in the following gender preferences through (often learned) perceptions:

Men

Power Base: Status and Independence.

Structure: Hierarchy.

Talk: Public (talks more at work)

Freedom: To maintain separateness.

Logic: Evaluates in a public sense, accepting the majority view as being the right one.

Style: Direct, maintaining power over others.

Emotions: Express anger, suppress anxieties.

Women

Power Base: Intimacy.

Structure: A network of community.

Talk: Private (talks more at home)

Freedom: To maintain connectedness.

Logic: Evaluates in a private sense. Personal experiences can negate a majority view.

Style: Indirect, by maintaining relationships.

Emotions: Suppress anger, express anxieties.

Women and men have characteristically different conversational styles, usually formed in childhood.

Women are more likely to phrase their preferences as polite suggestions, appearing to give others options in deciding what to do. Frequently these statements begin with, "Let's try...," or "Why don't we...," followed by their recommendations.

Men, on the other hand, tend to be more direct, phrasing statements more as commands, believing that indirect requests are manipulative, bordering on being dishonest.

To illustrate this phenomenon, let's say that a woman manager needs to have something done. She asks a male subordinate to do it; days later it still isn't done. What happened? This was their thinking:

Woman: She said, "The bookkeeper needs help with the billing. What would you think about helping her out?" She felt she had given him an implied command.

Man: He said, "OK," thinking, "OK, I'll consider helping her out." After he had thought about it, he decided he couldn't spare the time. He heard a suggestion he was free to reject.

Other aspects of women's conversational styles which weaken their impact with men are the higher pitch of their voices, which sound less authoritative, and women's tendencies to use disclaimers, such as "I don't know if this will work, but..." or "You've probably already thought of this, but..." In addition, women often speak in lower volume, with short statements (in order to appear succinct). Women wish to show consideration and invite response, but are interpreted by men as being uncertain and insecure.

How do these tendencies translate into communication strategies? Here's what they say:

Men would like women to:

- Be more direct and to the point.

- Stay focused and on the same subject.

- Keep in mind the "big picture."

- Be more objective. Not take things personally and not be petty (especially about other women).

- Be aware of male ego and not gang up on men, patronize them or try to dominate them.

Women would like men to:

- Take more time to listen, develop rapport and relationships.

- Evaluate issues from a broader spectrum before making a decision.

- Recognize that details can be important.

- Allow freer expression of emotion. Feelings are an important part of life and need to be addressed.

- Mentor women in achieving a view from the top.

By recognizing the inclinations of each other, and respecting each other's points of view, we can learn to be flexible and accommodate each other's needs. There is value in each gender's perspective. The extreme degree at either end of the spectrum is rarely a wise position. And, of course, the world is made up of individuals with unique combinations of these traits. Nevertheless, that delicate balance—so hard to achieve—is a worthy aspiration. The Multicultural Communication Model can help, incorporating the cultures of gender.

* * *

WOMEN IN BUSINESS: A CULTURAL CHANGE

This following is based on an article by the author originally published in December of 1994.

Recent data reflect the growing impact of women in U.S. business:

> More people are employed by women-owned businesses than by the Fortune 500 (**Working Woman** May 1993). 71% had been in business at least 9 years as of a 1992 study by the **National Association of Women Business Owners.**
>
> Women held 46% of nonclerical white-collar jobs reported to the **EEOC** in 1992.
>
> 57.8% of women 16 years and older are represented in the work force (**Bureau of Labor Statistics** November 1993). They are projected to reach 63.2% by the year 2005.

Nevertheless:

> Only 6% of the Fortune 500 have women directors on their boards (**Catalyst** 1993).
>
> Women held less than 1/3 of managerial jobs reported to the **EEOC** in 1992.

15.1% of all males in the work force are managers, while 7.5% of all women are managers (**The Wall Street Journal** March 29, 1994).

Despite the significance of these facts, women continue to make slow progress in the overall management ranks of U.S. organizations. Reasons for this slow growth rate are often rooted in deep-seated cultural values, which traditionally have defined men as directors and women as supporters. As long as these values rule organizations, women will continue to have difficulty breaking the so-called "glass ceiling" to upper management levels.

Culture change is required for our economic survival. In a survey published by **The Wall Street Journal** March 29, 1994, Rose Jonas, former personnel manager at Monsanto Company, said: "If the culture doesn't change, nothing will change for women." Jack Hall, vice president of employee relations at Ford Motor Company, agreed: "If we don't change the culture, we're not going to survive."

By focusing on successful models where change **is** occurring, however gradually, we can gain insight toward developing a new culture with a more balanced view of genders in the workplace. Let's start with two more companies cited in the above study.

Sara Lee Corporation was unwilling to wait for women's progress through the ranks. Beginning in the 1980's, they began hiring women into high-level jobs and watched the cultural changes trickle down. "The more women in top management jobs, the more women are attracted to them," says Gary Grom, senior vice president of human resources. These changes required a firm commitment from Chairman John Bryan, former civil rights activist who became Sara Lee's CEO in 1976. He notes, "We are the largest company in the world named for a woman, a distinction we are proud of. It gives us responsibility to be ahead of the curve on women's issues." Besides, he added, "Since one of our product lines is Hanes panty hose, it didn't make sense to have a bunch of old men sitting around trying to figure out the business."

Wells Fargo & Co. was found to have the greatest percentage of women in management at 66% in 1992. (This reflects a trend in the financial industry, which averages the highest employment of women managers at 41%.) In the 1980's Wells Fargo had many mergers and acquisitions. Women had an opportunity to show they could handle large projects and seemed to thrive in the company's decentralized, nonhierarchical structure.

This latter example supports findings of another study funded by The Society of Human Resource Management and reported in the February 1994 edition of **Training & Development.** Leadership styles of successful male and female small business owners were examined. They found that male and female employers did not differ significantly in personal characteristics and personnel practices. On the other hand, female managers had better track records for hiring women and their employees in general were happier with their jobs than were employees who worked for male owners. Also, contrary to popular opinion, women enjoyed working for other women. Both male and female employees reported similar positive levels of job satisfaction. Younger, better-educated males in particular, appeared to enjoy working for female employers.

Riane Eisler, author of **The Chalice and the Blade: Our History, Our Future**, identifies two basic kinds of corporate structures. The first, which she defines as the "dominator" model, is patterned after the military system and is largely hierarchical. The second, the "partnership" model, stresses cooperation and collaboration. She suggests that this second model, which is gradually replacing the first, is ideal for the woman manager whose skills traditionally have flourished in this type of setting.

Sally Helgesen, in her book **The Female Advantage**, compares the two models to games learned as children. Men have historically used football as a business model, with its organizational structure, tenacious focus on objective, concentration on blocking the competition, emphasis on deployment of efficient units, and requirement that team players do what they're told and not question the coach. Girls, on the other hand, have preferred more interpersonal games, such as hopscotch, house, dolls, jump rope, all emphasizing cooperation and role-playing. These more flexible games prepared women to improvise, concentrating more on the process than the goal. The ability to respond quickly to changing business conditions is becoming an increasingly valuable trait in today's world.

It is interesting to compare these studies with anecdotal data derived from one of our recent workshops. A group of women defined "women as a cultural group" as "sensitive, adaptable, determined, having fortitude and emotional strength, doers with a high work ethic, nurturing and caring, open, communicative, confrontive in a positive sense and having integrity." Conversely, a group of men defined "men as a cultural group" as "confident, aggressive, head of the family (including finances), open to change, involved in sports, a hero, we 'fix' things, run the company and the country, are leaders, decision makers, successful, and bond with other males."

So, it could be said that *the successful culture model we seek of bringing male and female perspectives into balance will create an organization:*

- Whose structure is fluid and can adapt quickly to change,

- Where directiveness is tempered with strong interpersonal skills,

- Where process is defined through consensus-building collaboration, and

- Growth opportunities are provided equally to women and men.

Key to achieving this goal is understanding communication between genders. Deborah Tannen, in her book **You Just Don't Understand,** asserts that men value independence over intimacy, while women value connection over status. These values were learned as children, according to her studies of Americans raised before the 70's. (Since then, boys and girls have been taught more similar values in the U.S., although recent studies indicate that the old messages are still being learned subliminally.) In addition, since men often associate intimacy with sex, they can misinterpret the efforts of women to establish an "intimate" or genuine relationship with a co-worker. This difference in interpretation can lead to mixed signals and sexual harassment complications. Other gender-based communication differences can occur through the use of language, boundaries, and power, all of which experts agree are very similar to the gaps occurring among different ethnic cultures. Periodic training in cultural (including gender) communication can ease strains due to these differences, but ongoing organizational policy changes need to reinforce the culture change.

Judith Tingley, author of **Genderflex: Ending the Workplace War Between the Sexes,** points out that an effective interpersonal strategy is "to temporarily use communication behaviors typical of the other gender in order to increase potential for influence." Beth Milwid interviewed successful businesswomen for their strategies in **Working With Men**. One manager says that she acts like a man in the boardroom, where male traditions of military leadership still rule, but with staff she uses participatory management.

At the current rate, women will not achieve parity with male managers for another 20-30 years. Can we afford to wait? The opportunities open for U.S. business could multiply rapidly through more effective utilization of its female work force. The sooner cultural change produces a workplace environment where women can fully realize their potential, the sooner prosperity will expand.

* * *

"Some of us are becoming the men we wanted to marry."

Gloria Steinem

MULTICULTURAL COMMUNICATION STRATEGIES

CHAPTER 4

Cultural Compendium

This cultural collection is designed to provide "food for thought" as you study the complexities of multicultural perceptions, and reflect on our many common interests.

White males are typically presumed to be competent unless proved otherwise. Minorities and women are presumed to be incompetent until proved otherwise.

It is rude in East Asian cultures to answer a question in the negative. People will say "yes" even if they mean "no," to show respect.

Hispanics are raised with the notion that if you are good, someone will know about it. You never talk about yourself.
Santiago Rodriguez, Apple Computer

European accents are usually viewed favorably in America, while Vietnamese or Cantonese accents often cause a negative response.

Respect for authority, modesty and harmony are three values Asians hold dear.

While the Asians have a greater acceptance of authority of supervisors, in Scandinavia the subordinate

and manager hold almost equal power. U.S. managers are about in the middle of the range.
King Ming Young, Hewlett-Packard

Compare these cultural proverbs: "The nail that sticks out will get hammered down." (Eastern) "The squeaky wheel gets the grease." (Western)

The Chinese are taught to not challenge elders, confront people or speak until your thoughts are fully developed. I must continually fight these tendencies in an American management setting where open communication is encouraged and brainstorming is a standard technique in decision-making.

Many Israelies believe that if you don't argue in a negotiation, it's not fun.
Albert Yu, VP & General Manager, Intel

Blacks and Hispanics approach situations with a more feeling, caring manner, while white men often approach them with a man-to-object manner. To a Black, "feeling" is all-important, and if a white manager comes off non-caring, the Black will construe racism, even when it's not. Then you have rebellion.
Cle Jackson, Wang Laboratories

We learn grammar of the English language because English for us is a tool to be used. But the Japanese language is part of the experience to be lived.
Edward C. Stewart, **Communique,** *SIETAR*

Many black males feel they do not have to look at each other when speaking, or nod their heads or make occasional conversational noise to show they are

listening. An absence of these dominant cultural traits can be misunderstood by whites as being rude, dishonest, uninterested or even hostile.
Harry Waters, Jr., California State

Puerto Ricans in a San Juan coffee shop will touch each other 180 times an hour; Britons in a London pub will not touch at all.
Bernard Asbell, **What They Know About You.**

U.S. managers who switch coasts must adapt to different approaches to the use of time.
Joan E. Rigdon, **Wall Street Journal**

An employee from Southeast Asia did not understand it was acceptable to talk to co-workers on the job. Consequently, each time his supervisor spoke to him, even if just to say, "Good Morning," the employee thought he was being singled out for not working hard enough.
Steve Hanamura, Consultant

In our society, even the Japanese can be outsiders, but the ultimate outsider is the foreigner.

More important than religion, or ideology, perfection to us is almost an aesthetic sense, deep in our culture and hard for others to imitate.
Shuichi Kato, Japanese Social Critic

Americans are task oriented. Follow-through is relationship oriented. An American supervisor, Roger, gave a Japanese employee, Watanabe-san, a job, saying "I want you to finish this for me and give me a report

three weeks from Friday at 3:00 p.m." Watanabe-san agreed to meet the deadline. Three weeks go by. When the time came, the report did not arrive. Roger angrily went to Watanabe-san asking why the report was not finished. "Well, sir, I did not think it was any longer important, since I have not heard from you in three weeks. I thought perhaps there were other priorities I should have been putting my time on." Watanabe expected Roger would come by frequently to check on the status of the report and to see if any additional help was needed. From Watanabe's point of view, the fact that follow-up wasn't there indicated a lack of commitment to the relationship.
Clifford Clarke, **Cultural Diversity at Work**

Barriers to communication prevent meanings from meeting.
Reuel Howe

From the research perspective, I am encouraged by the recent and more empirically rigorous studies which suggest that a strong cultural/ethnic identity (ingroup identification) makes one feel more secure and therefore more open to outgroup members. Social identity theory also explains the mechanism in which new identities can emerge....The development of this kind of global identity represents an **additional** group identification; not a replacement of one's cultural ethnic group identity.
Mitchell R. Hammer, Ph.D., **Communique,** *SIETAR*

The central thesis of my book (**Managing on the Edge**) is that adaptive organizations build a great deal of **contention** within themselves, and they use it constructively....You can value differences in an organization and among people as a source of creativity, as a spur to causing people to rethink their assumptions.
Richard Pascale, ***Industry Week***

He has the right to criticize who has the heart to help.
Abraham Lincoln

Style in and of itself is not good or bad. It's effective or it's ineffective. When all else fails, remember that you are there to achieve results, and that various styles should be seen as tools to be applied to the key purpose at hand.
Andrew S. Grove, CEO, Intel

A heterogeneous community of individuals and groups with different skills, experience, and characteristics is better able to adapt to changing circumstances than one that is homogeneous....In a community of people with different talents, skills, and resources, someone is always present to do for another what the other cannot do alone. This is the safeguard of human diversity. This is the refracted and reflected beauty of a multitude.
Prof. Charles Willie, Harvard University

Anger is only one letter short of danger.
Harvey Mackay

Every part of our culture comes from the earth....In our culture, the universe is man....Man is a part of the natural world. There is not one world for man and one for animals, they are part of the same one and lead parallel lives....Maize is the center of our universe.

We Indians never do anything which goes against the laws of our ancestors...which say we should love everything that exists....(We) must never steal or abuse the natural world, or show disrespect for any living thing.
Rigoberta Menchu, ***An Indian Woman in Guatemala,*** *(Nobel Peace Prize Winner)*

Prejudice survives all evidence.
Wynton Marsalis, attributed to Richard Wagner

When you meet people, no matter what opinion you might have formed about them beforehand, why, after you meet them and see their angle and their personality, why, you can see a lot of good in all of them.
Will Rogers

Iranians are known in Los Angeles as being hard bargainers—they always want to negotiate everything.
"All Things Considered," ***National Public Radio,*** *March 1995*

Two Americans chatting in a coffee shop in Gainesville, Florida, will touch each other twice an hour. If they're Parisians in a cafe on the Champs-Elysees, they'll touch about 100 times an hour; Puerto Ricans in

a San Juan coffee shop, 180 times. But Britons in a London pub will touch not at all.
Bernard Asbell, **What They Know About You**

American communication style is like a basketball game: everybody chasing—and interrupting—each other. To be effective in foreign negotiations Americans need to slow down, shut up and listen.
Morio Itozu, Tokyo Consultant

There are no more age norms, which is why people feel so dislocated....But some of the things that seem quite unnatural now will become more natural.
Gail Sheehy, **New Passages** *(1995)*

The ancient Greeks were about the first people to let go of the idea that a culture is a matter of being born in a certain ethnic or racial group. They were willing to accept as Greeks some who lived in quite different places...They could be Greek if they spoke the Greek language and had some traditions which were Greek. So there, culture is being defined as certain habits, certain behaviors which we can understand as certain traditions using a certain code, the language, certain ways of life, rather than to be defined as ethnicity or language or where one lives.

The Germans originated the idea of economics driving society, rather than politics, in the 1870's.
Edward C. Stewart

If you lose the power to laugh, you lose the power to think.
Clarence Darrow

We used to be taught we were losing nerve cells every day....We're beginning to get very good evidence that there is not a lot of neuronal (brain cell) loss with age.
Marilyn Albert, M.D., Harvard Professor & Director of Gerontology Research at Massachusetts General Hospital - September 1994

There isn't much difference between a 25-year-old brain and a 75-year-old brain....Education and interesting work serve as a kind of vaccination to protect people against Alzheimer's disease.
*Monte S. Buchsbaum, M.D.,
Dir. of Neuroscience Laboratory
Mt. Sinai School of Medicine, New York*

There is a strong parallel in stories of each culture in terms of fate, and cause and effect, of man being responsible for his conscience, and how the hero is affected by outside events. Call it Eastern, call it Western. The through-line is universal.
Elizabeth Sung, Chinese-American actor

In politics, if you want anything said, ask a man. If you want anything done, ask a woman.
Margaret Thatcher

Where everyone thinks alike, no one thinks very much.
Walter Lippmann

* * *

CHAPTER 5

THE MULTICULTURAL U.S. MARKETPLACE

The preceding sections of this book have examined how we all are multicultural. A significant application of this knowledge is in the U.S. marketplace, and how we can be more effective with our customers. The following sections explore the nature of the diverse American marketplace and some applications of multicultural awareness in customer relations. They are based on the author's previously published articles.

A GROWING CUSTOMER FOCUS: CULTURAL DIVERSITY

More and more U.S. businesses are discovering that "multicultural sells." This quote appeared in a November 24, 1993, article in **The Wall Street Journal**, which cites a Schick commercial showing faces of different races dissolving into each other. A later ad in the same publication (March 14, 1994) used a black manager from Eastman Kodak Company to promote **People** magazine, "The Book That Reads America.^{SM}" Allstate Insurance began diversifying the "good hands" in its TV spots in 1991. These items illustrate one approach to multicultural advertising: that whites and minorities can be reached by the same ads, as long as a variety of cultures is represented in the ads. Other advertisers prefer marketing directly to specific cultural groups, which requires accuracy. For example, an Asian advertising executive in California noted, "The mistake most advertisers make is thinking that all Asians are homogeneous." To avoid stereotyping, marketers often need to differentiate among the five major Asian groups of Japanese, Korean, Chinese, Vietnamese and Filipino.

To further support this niche marketing strategy, consider these figures: as of August 1994, 60 million African-Americans, Asian-Americans and Hispanics resided in the U.S. and wielded $580 billion worth of annual buying power, according to **Home Office Computing.**

Let's look at several business segments and identify how addressing cultural diversity in the U.S. marketplace is contributing to the direct profitability of numerous organizations today.

Retail

"What's in store for retail developers? Ethnic marketplaces." So goes the headline of a November 22, 1992, **Chicago Tribune** article regarding inner city shopping centers in Los Angeles, such as Koreatown Plaza and Baldwin Hills/Crenshaw Plaza, which targets African-American shoppers.

"Black consumers have strong economic muscle, but they have been underserved in their local markets," states Jeffrey Humphreys, a University of Georgia economist. To meet this demand, an Atlanta mall restyled itself to an "Afrocentric retail center."

John Kozlowski, Senior Vice President of Human Resources at Kinney Shoe Corporation, states "Today's retail environment needs a diverse work force to service a diverse customer base." Through training and hiring, Kinney seeks to ensure that commitment. Montgomery Ward & Co. has welcomed Latino shoppers by several means, including (1) naming the host of a top-rated Spanish-language talk show as a company spokesperson; (2) offering scholarships to Hispanics; and (3) customizing some stores with Spanish-in-store signs and Spanish-speaking customer service representatives. Ward's chairman, Bernard F. Brennan, said, "Hispanics are this country's most dynamic and fastest-growing population group." Hispanics constitute more than 50 percent of the customers in 30 of the company's 360 stores.

With men becoming more active in parenting and homemaking, manufacturers of household products recognize they need to advertise cross-gender. Johnson & Johnson has ads showing a "man's man" rolling a shopping cart down a supermarket aisle with baby in tow. In 1991 men purchased 32% of frozen food, 27% detergent, 30% soup, 30% cold remedies, 24% baby food, 21% baking mixes and 40% bottled water.

The pianomaker Steinway & Sons began seeing more Asians in its Manhattan showroom. Recognizing that Asians value brand names, musical culture and education, they hired Chinese and Korean-speaking sales people and devised special Asian family ads saying "A Lifelong Gift for Your Child and a Great Investment for Dad." In 1991 Asians bought 15 percent of all pianos purchased in North America.

When Coca-Cola developed recent network TV spots, they used Burrell Advertising, a firm which for 20 years has been Coke's agency for ads targeting black consumers. The new spots portray young blacks as avowed individualists and trendsetters proud of their style and appearance, values which were defined in a major research study. The study also revealed that 87 percent of those African-Americans surveyed believe that "anyone can be successful in this country if they are willing to work hard," and 66 percent said "You should never use being black as an excuse for your problems." Trendsetting individuality is equally prized. "People should feel free to look, dress and live the way they want," said 86 percent of the blacks surveyed. It was also found that religion and a sense of duty play even bigger roles in the lives of blacks than for non-blacks. Charles Curry, president of Burrell Advertising, said "Black consumers want to be included in advertising, and they want to be portrayed fairly, positively and realistically....Once you understand a group's value set, what they hold important, you can explain almost everything that group does."

In the clothing line, Levi Strauss & Co. has long recognized that promoting diversity in the work force makes good marketing sense. "It's tough to design and develop merchandise for markets you don't understand," says Dan Chew, manager of corporate marketing. Today Levi is recognized as among the most ethnically and culturally diverse companies in the U.S., if not the world.

Two newcomers to the field are Threads 4 Life, one of the first apparel companies to sell directly to the black community, and Mothers Work, selling upscale maternity clothes for working mothers-to-be. The founders of each company were recognized by Fortune Magazine in its March 21, 1994, edition as being among young entrepreneurs whose organizations generated $17 billion in sales during 1993 and which created nearly 64,000 jobs.

Long before others in their industry, Threads 4 Life founders, T. J. Walker and Carl Jones, saw that multiculturalism could pay. "Black kids are setting the trends in fashion. Because they don't have much money to buy cars or stereos, they believe that clothes give them their identity." About 40% of its clothes are bought by blacks; the rest by mostly white suburban teens who "think it's cool to mimic the black culture." The clothes have also been strong sellers in Europe and Japan.

Civil engineer Rebecca Matthias needed stylish maternity clothes to wear to work. Sensing that other women had the same problem, she began making and selling them through her Mothers Work company. In 1993 she opened 51 new stores, for a total of 113, with plans for additional expansion.

Toys are another area where multiculturalism has expanded sales. Cultural Toys, the nation's first African-American-owned full-line toy firm, is a $3 billion company. The toys are carried by such giant chains as Wal-Mart, FAO Schwarz (who bought the entire line), Dayton Hudson Corporation and Kay Bee Toys, the nation's mall-based toy retailer. The company's founder, Jacob Miles III, wanted to be in a market segment driven by the mother, rather than the child, with a message of non-violence and multiculturalism.

In a February 1994 report, of the 56.8 million children under 14 in the U.S., nearly 15 percent were black, more than 13 percent Hispanic and more than 3 percent Asian; 67 percent were white. In a little more than 15 years the number of kids under age 14 is expected to grow to nearly 60.5 million, of which nearly 19 percent will be Hispanic, 16 percent black and more than 6 percent Asian, while 58 percent will be white.

These figures help explain why the multicultural playroom now has diverse dolls. African-Americans have expressed the greatest interest in dolls in their images, spending $749 million on toys and games in 1992. There is Kenya, The Beautiful Hairstyling Doll, who comes with beads for cornrowing her hair and is available in three African-American skin tones. There is Jennifer, wearing a tag printed in English and Spanish, and Consuelo, a Hispanic fashion doll. There are Kulture Kids, packaged with a map of Africa, and Hip Hop Kids, a culturally diverse collection of doll friends including characters named B-Boy Smart, Puerto Rick and Girlfriend.

Another company produces a line of American Girls Collection dolls, books, clothes and accessories. The first non-white doll in the series is about Addy Walker, developed by black novelist Connie Porter and an advisory board of black historians, museum curators educators and other experts. The materials trace Addy's fictional life from slavery in the South to freedom in Philadelphia.

Computers

"Women Are the Focus of a PC Maker," headlines an October 7, 1993, marketing article in **The Wall Street Journal**. In its Compaq commercial, the personal computer company states "Traditionally, there's been a direct correlation between megahertz and testosterone." Now the Houston-based giant's largest advertising campaign ever recognizes that women are already the primary personal computer users in a quarter of all American homes with PCs. In addition, women traditionally control the household budget and are primarily responsible for the after-hours education of children.

In a March 1994 series in the same publication an analysis was made of how genders use computers. Its message: women use PCs as tools, men as toys. Whereas women use them to get a job done, men use them for pleasure. The implications of computer usage are being studied by psychologists to further understand how men and women adapt to business conditions. Video games, usually dismissed by women as boring, can teach women cross-gender interpersonal and competitive strategies. New on-line services are being offered geared to the interests and preferences of women.

Financials

Financial institutions are discovering it pays to provide more services to women and minorities. Women-owned businesses employ more people than the Fortune 500, and are projected to account for 48 percent of all U.S. small businesses by 2000 (U.S. Census

Bureau, Small Business Administration). As a result lenders are making more loans and offering financial advice to women business owners. The ten best cities for women entrepreneurs in 1994 were centered in the northern Midwest, Northeast and southern California. In these regional areas women-owned businesses account for 29-34 percent of all firms, with revenues from $850 million to $15 billion. Representative businesses include: computer services, apparel manufacturing, health services, trucking, construction, car dealers, real estate, multi-lingual training, hospitality and retail.

The credit card industry has discovered that linking cards to ancestral affinity gives them an edge over the competition. Cards geared to the Irish, Latinos, Poles, African-Americans and Macedonians, among others, are now being offered by financial institutions. Another expression of cultural heritage is available to African-Americans via their bank checks. In 1990 Marshall Johnson recognized that, despite their $293 billion annual spending power, African-Americans were not represented on any of the U.S. currency. So he initiated a company which prints pictures of African-American historic figures on bank checks. The checks, called the African-American Heritage Check series, are now available in banks and credit unions throughout the United States.

Automobiles

Women buy 49 percent of all cars and influence nearly 80 percent of all buying decisions. Consequently, Ford recognized they needed to keep women's priorities in mind when designing vehicles. The 1992 redesigned

Probe model from Ford was specifically created with female drivers in mind. Developed by a woman-led task force, considerations were given to such realities as long nails, skirts, and driving in high heels. Midas Muffler is now courting women drivers with Project Baby Safe. Amoco Oil broke a 105-year old tradition when it geared its 1993 marketing campaign directly to women.

Our final example of paying attention to the female auto customer is provided by Chicago car dealers who have brought women salespersons into the showroom. Among the resulting super-seller strategies were: bringing toys into the showroom to occupy the attention of children while their mothers are reviewing the models; a salesperson driving models to the homes of potential buyers who are too pregnant to stop at the dealership; piling kids into the back of a showroom station wagon to demonstrate its versatility; and showing personal excitement at the benefits to be derived from a car. A dealership owner believes women salespersons could dominate the field, largely because of their people skills. "They make the customer feel like buying a car is an important event."

Entertainment

From radio and television, to musical recordings, to ethnic clubs, to the hospitality industry, to museums— cultural diversity is playing a significant part in the entertainment industry.

A spanish radio station in Los Angeles, KLAX, has been named by Arbitron as the most-listened-to station in the Los Angeles market, which is only one-third Hispanic. From 1990-1993 the number of Hispanic radio stations in the U.S. grew 21 percent. Advertisers spent $222.6 million to reach Hispanic radio audiences in 1992, a 6 percent gain over 1990. Included among the advertisers were more big-name consumer product companies such as Procter & Gamble, McDonald's and Coca-Cola. TV networks are now featuring more minority characters in many of their mainstream series, as well as creating on-going programs about specific cultural groups.

    Musical recordings are another area reflecting multiculturalism, through single heritages and new combinations of musical derivatives. A popular Texas musical style is called "Tejano," a style combining rock, blues and country. Disc jockeys often use a hybrid of English and Spanish that some call "Spanglish" in discussing the recordings. Another mix, combining "Rhythm, Country and Blues," features black (traditionally rhythm and blues) and country (traditionally white) performers in a public television special developed by megagiant MCA Records (a company now owned by the Japanese). The music was recorded in an album celebrating both forms of music in the same project, with artists from both genres performing every song.

    Ethnic nightclubs of Chicago represent the diverse traditions of communities found in the Chicago area. Samples are Arbela, Mesopotamian and Assyrian immigrants from Iraq; The Polonaise NightClub, Polish; The Abbey Pub, Irish-Americans; Deni's Den, Greek; and Zum Deutschen Eck, German. In one neighborhood, clubs reflecting the Polish, Hispanic and Gay community find their patrons are mixed. Said one recent Polish immigrant visiting the Hispanic club, "To tell you the truth, I've never been in a place like this. In Poland, we couldn't do this. But here in Chicago, in the U.S., people are more open."

Another driving force in Hispanic clubs is the Banda dance craze, the primary focus of clubs in California, Chicago, and Los Angeles. Musicologists say the music's greatest impact may be cultural, reflecting the newfound ethnic pride among Mexican-Americans. Banda dancers like to display their heritage in items of clothing, a practice which has spawned new clothing stores carrying these special wares. An ethnomusicology teacher at the University of California at Los Angeles says, "The **mestizo** (as Hispanics with mixed European and American-Indian ancestry are called) are reclaiming their past. You feel this void if you always keep avoiding your culture, so at one point or another, you're going to embrace it."

The hospitality industry is also taking notice of multicultural meeting planners representing groups with growing economic clout. Take for instance the black meetings and conventions market, spending $5 billion annually. African-American meeting planners are taking their business in increasing numbers to cities where blacks have management positions in hotels, convention bureaus and convention centers. As a result, convention bureau representatives are becoming more responsive to their needs and are actively courting more black meetings and conventions. In a 1993 survey of the National Coalition of Black Meeting Planners, cities which ranked high on their list were Washington, D.C., Atlanta, New York, St. Louis and Indianapolis. All except Indianapolis had black mayors and large African-American populations; Indianapolis, on the other hand, was praised for attentive service and aggressive recruitment of minority meetings, reasonable rates, safety and a good convention center.

Conventioneers are also finding that the museums in their host cities are becoming more reflective of diverse cultures. "People come to museums where people see themselves in the walls, whether it is in art, history or science," says recent president of the American Association of Museums, Ellsworth Brown. Museum programs include not only diverse works of art, but also lectures and bus tours through ethnic neighborhoods; informal workshops focused on different ethnic communities; brochures printed in several languages; ongoing lectures on Hispanic and African studies; and community programs such as "Neighbors Night," publicized in flyers in English, Spanish and Chinese.

These are just a few examples of how multiculturalism is enriching the U.S. marketplace, not only through the recognition of diverse customers and demands for goods and services, but also through new paradigms for future growth possibilities. A wealth of opportunity awaits the cultural visionary.

* * *

MULTICULTURAL CUSTOMER RELATIONS

As the U.S. population becomes increasingly heterogeneous, organizations are faced with a growing demand to provide multicultural customer service. Not only are customers more diverse, but employees who serve them also represent a wide variety of cultural heritages. In the face of this challenge, global communication techniques are required to succeed.

Today, because both sellers and buyers are diverse, customer relations strategies need to incorporate (1) how our own backgrounds may affect our attitudes toward customers, and (2) how the values of our customers may affect their interactions with us, the sellers. We will now examine two actual case histories from our archives and discuss how cultural factors contributed to misunderstanding and customer dissatisfaction. Recommendations for prevention and positive action follow.

(It should be noted that these examples are neither intended to convey all cultural values of any one group, nor to suggest that these attitudes would be valid in every case; due to our unique life experiences we all have different degrees of acculturation. Rather, these histories are meant to illustrate what **may** occur, based on frequent cultural learnings.)

CASE STUDY ONE

You (the buyer) walk into your local bank and, when it is your turn in line, find a young Asian woman behind the teller's cage. You are a little annoyed, because she does not acknowledge your presence by looking at you or saying anything. Feeling ignored you finally ask, "Are you available?" She glances briefly at you, then looks down and says, "Yes," maintaining her expressionless demeanor. You hand her your paperwork and she processes the transaction, never looking at you and remaining silent. When finished she lays your receipt on the counter, being careful not to touch you in the process. (You think to yourself, "She acts like I'm diseased or something, like I'm not good enough to touch!") You leave the bank feeling frustrated and rebuffed by the lack of interpersonal exchange you have come to expect. After all, the bank wouldn't be in business without you, the customer, and they should act more appreciative! If this keeps up you just may take your business elsewhere. Who needs to be treated like you're invisible. You want your bank to treat you like a person, not a machine.

Analysis One

The customer's acculturation was typical of many with Anglo-American expectations, as well as those of African-Americans, some Hispanics and some Europeans. This customer (a middle-aged Anglo-American woman) expected at minimum direct eye contact, a welcoming "Hello" from the bank representative, a pleasant smile and probably a closing phrase, such as "Have a good day." This personal attention would have conveyed to the customer that the **bank** acknowledged the person's value as an individual and as a customer. To not have received what the customer perceived as the barest courtesy was insulting to the person's dignity and sense of self-esteem—every person's right in the customer's value system.

From the teller's point of view (a first-generation Korean immigrant), she had been taught by her family that it was inappropriate, even rude, to look at someone directly if she wanted to convey respect to that person.

Smiling would also have been out of place, as in her culture this is a very familiar gesture and should be used only with close friends and family; emotional expressions should be contained in public. Her group orientation resulted in her not wanting to stand out or call attention to herself, so she waited for the customer to initiate the transaction. Her silence was also respectful, since she had learned that to honor seniority, young women particularly should be careful about calling attention to themselves. In addition, her values included honoring people's sense of personal space, and she perceived touching would have been an invasion of that territory, as well as excessively familiar. She felt she was fulfilling her job responsibilities adequately by devoting her attention solely to processing the transaction, and that to engage in conversation with the bank's customers would have been overstepping her authority.

CASE STUDY TWO

You (the seller) are making a follow-up call to a middle-aged African-American man who has recently received his first order of your widgets. You want to make sure everything was all right with the shipment and try to establish an ongoing relationship with this new customer. Once it has been clarified that the widgets were satisfactory, you think about how you can build rapport with him. You are uncomfortable with the way he looks at you and wonder if he dislikes you. On the other hand, when you were explaining some new features of your product line, you felt frustrated because he was looking everywhere but at you, so you weren't sure if he had understood or, for that matter, was even interested. He gave no sign that you had "connected" with him.

Trying to find some common ground you observe photographs on his credenza. You ask him if they are of his family. He pauses a moment, and answers "Yes." Thinking you are on the right track to establish a relationship, you ask him some questions about his family. The more you query him, the quieter he gets and then suddenly he says he has to terminate the meeting due to another commitment. You think to yourself, "What did I do wrong? I was just trying to show interest in him as a person and then demonstrate our common concerns by telling him about my family. In my culture, family always comes first. He acts like I insulted him or something. Why was he so hostile?"

Analysis Two

The attitudes of the seller (a young Hispanic male) reflect values often learned by Latinos, as well as common strategies taught by Anglo-American sales strategists. Hispanics often learn respect for authority within a hierarchical framework and thus will use eye contact with discretion, i.e., establishing eye contact but looking away periodically. Black men, on the other hand, often have different conversational modes, e.g., when they do look at others it can be perceived as direct and deliberate; at the same time, they do not necessarily feel required to look at the speaker, respond with conversational noises like "Hm-Hmm" or nod their heads occasionally to acknowledge that they are listening. A strategy for the seller in this kind of situation could be to ask open-ended indirect questions periodically which would require the buyer to paraphrase his understanding and, if there is confusion, the seller can clarify.

In many Hispanic cultures, where family takes high priority, it is proper protocol and considerate to raise family issues as a basis for establishing a business relationship. A variation of that in sales training is to nurture the customer relationship by expressing interest in him as a person first, followed by business dealings. African-American men, however, may consider personal questions by relative strangers to be intrusive and disrespectful. The seller could make comments of a more general nature, allowing the buyer flexibility to choose how personally revealing his responses will be.

GENERAL COMMENTS AND RECOMMENDATIONS

In each of the above cases it is clear that the employers needed to emphasize that the employees' job responsibilities included paying attention to customers' needs. Multicultural sensitivity training will alert these employees to what their customers' concerns are. Communication skills should be practiced. Then, by using their powers of observation and communicative skills, they can modify their behavior to meet the expectations of multicultural customers, thus insuring more positive customer relations in the future.

* * *

"The more you know about the nuances and details of the Asian-American culture, the easier it is to penetrate the market....Although there are universal concepts and themes that apply to all Asian-Americans, U.S. businesses that home in on this group's diversity of customs and (more than 16) sub-cultures will get the most attention and loyalty."

Jennie Tong, Owner
Lee Liu & Tong (LLT) advertising agency, NYC

CHAPTER 6

INTERNATIONAL PHILOSOPHIES & PROTOCOL

Visitors to the U.S. and international business collaborators say that Americans often share certain traits. Let's review a few condensed quotes from these non-Americans, then examine some perspectives in their countries...particularly with respect to business protocol. (As you review these, remember Step 1 of the Communication Model, reminding us that individuals reflect varying degrees of their home country cultures.)

USA

◘ Americans appear warm and friendly, but if a relationship starts to get personal, they avoid it. They like to keep business and personal matters separate.

◘ Americans always ask, "How are you" and then never stop to find out. Similarly, they say "Let's have lunch" or "Let's get together sometime" and then don't follow up.

◘ Americans display emotions openly and in public. In higher business dealings, however, emotions are usually contained.

◘ Americans smile to show friendship or agreement.

◘ Americans joke around a lot, using humor loosely. Getting too serious seems to be a sign of weakness. The ultimate compliment is an insult, particularly among men.

◘ Americans like to be direct and come to the point right away. They can be impatient for short-term rewards.

◘ Americans are uncomfortable with silence and may become uneasy waiting for responses. They view hesitancy as a sign of uncertainty or being indecisive which, for them, is a negative.

◘ With Americans, results count more than how you get there.

◘ Americans tend to publicize their accomplishments. They accept praise as their due.

◘ Americans seem to think speed is everything. In their efforts to beat the competition, they may rush their proposals just to get the main concept to the foreign party as quickly as possible, thinking they can correct any mistakes later.

◘ Americans do not fear rejection too much, thinking they can always come back with a better plan.

◘ Americans have a strong work ethic and are highly task-oriented, sometimes to the detriment of relationships. The job usually takes priority over family interests.

◘ Anglo-American parents teach their children to be independent and self-reliant. They believe the most important aspect of intelligence is cognitive ability—problem-solving and being creative.

International - General
(External to USA)

◘ Generally speaking, a good strategy to follow is to think of yourself as a "guest" when visiting someone else's country and, as such, the rules of the host apply.

◘ Business is never conducted over the telephone. "Telemarketing," as it is known in the U.S., is abhorred. In many countries comparisons to other products/services is illegal, even to claiming "best" in ads.

◘ Guard against answering overseas telephone calls with the phrase, "What can I do for you." Most other countries prefer a more indirect style, starting out with some preliminary conversation about personal matters before getting down to business.

◘ Never rely on local postal or telephone service. Important documents should be sent by international courier firms. Faxing is often best for routine correspondence, or computerized E-Mail.

◘ Correspondence from strangers is likely to be ignored.

◘ Long-term personal relationships are at the base of most business ventures. Time is relative to the overall objective and the culture's priorities.

◘ Written contracts may or may not be binding.

◘ Introductions and referrals are essential in most international business negotiations. Local partners can provide a cross-cultural bridge.

◘ Business cards should clearly identify the individual's education, position and role in the organization.

◘ Behave and dress conservatively. Learn local customs regarding gifts, colors, good table manners, written "thank-you" notes.

◘ Speak as much as you can of the local language; it will be appreciated. Non-verbal communication, such as demeanor, carries messages.

◘ Be prepared for the language difference. Always ask permission first to speak in English. Be prepared with a translator. Try to speak some of the local language; it will be appreciated.

◘ Avoid admiring specific objects as the host may feel obligated to make it yours as a courtesy and sign of proper breeding.

◘ In countries conditioned to monopolistic regimes, such as Russia and China, service workers may ignore customers or say, "Ask someone else," or "If you're not buying what are you looking at..." As competition becomes more prevalent in their economies, customers are beginning to be treated more kindly.

Body Language

◘ Shake hands upon arrival and departure, starting with the most senior person. Business women should initiate the handshake with men. Never end a meeting without a handshake. A firm handshake can signal aggressiveness in the Middle East and Europe.

◘ It is not uncommon to see two men walking hand-in-hand in public in Japan, China and Arab countries.

◘ The "A-OK" sign, thumb and forefinger forming a circle, is an obscene gesture in Mexico and Germany.

◘ In South America and Japan people beckon each other with their palms down.

◘ The thumbs-up gesture is an inflammatory obscenity in Australia and parts of West Africa.

Europe

◘ European business people want to check business credentials carefully before entering into a business relationship.

◘ In Europe, one has the "regal right" to protect individual personal information.

◘ Exact titles are *very* important. In Germany titles accumulate, such as "Herr Doktor Geshaftsfuhrer" (Mr. Doctor President). They do not necessarily represent the function performed.

◘ Europeans dislike breakfast, lunch or dinner meetings. They prefer to keep business and pleasure separate.

◘ Northern European countries are more formal and conservative, less so near the Mediterranean. Office greetings to staff are customary.

◘ Superlatives are viewed suspiciously. Understatement is valued.

◘ In the U.K., to "table" a topic means to bring it into open discussion.

◘ Italians find Americans too much in a hurry, not taking enough time to talk with their Italian colleagues, and too combative.

◘ Humor in business dealings in Germany is considered inappropriate.

◘ In France, direct questions are considered rude. An indirect approach is preferred, e.g., "Excuse me, I have a problem."

◘ Guests in Europe bring either cut flowers (an uneven number and never red roses) or a box of chocolates for the hostess. Gift wrappings are symbolic; avoid white, red and brown, which have negative connotations in some countries. No wrappings on cut flowers.

Body Language

◘ Men, women and children all shake hands, one quick pump.

◘ In England, Scotland and Sardinia tapping the side of the nose means, "You and I are in on the secret." If a Welshman does it, however, he means, "You're really nosy."

◘ The "V" sign with knuckles turned out is England's equivalent of the American middle finger.

◘ The hand wave with palms exposed in Greece could be misinterpreted as, "Go to Hell." Greeks wave with the backs of their hands.

◘ Tapping the temple signifies something or someone is crazy except in Holland, where the gesture means, "How clever!"

◘ Appropriate kisses on the cheek: Zero to one in Britain, two on most of the Continent, three in Belgium and French-speaking Switzerland, and four in Paris.

◘ Excessive smiling is perceived as being dim-witted and condescending in France. Smiles have to be earned. A serious, even funereal, expression is usually most appropriate. Subtle messages are conveyed with the eyes.

Latin America

◘ Personal relationships are essential to successful business ventures and are usually established before business is conducted. Business relationships are built on trust between people, rather than organizations.

◘ Social ranking in the society is significant.

◘ The external environment is viewed as alien to the family; therefore little effort is made to control it.

◘ Mexicans can be wary of outsiders.

◘ Mexicans have a sense of humor, even about death. But not in advertising.

◘ Manana means soon as well as tomorrow.

◘ In Mexico it is common to have long lunch breaks, often to nourish business relationships, then to return to the office and work late.

◘ Family relationships are supreme in Mexico; business commitments take lower priority than family obligations.

◘ Although Mexico's increasing internationalization is causing business to be more prompt, Mexicans are still likely to look at a delay as fate, and believe little can be done about it.

◘ Time is relative in Mexico. Meetings often start late. Foreign business interests may want to build time cushions into deadlines, and make low-key friendly progress calls.

◘ In Mexico, avoid office visits in the afternoon or near holidays.

◘ Style and presentation are important. Dress in high-quality, conservative apparel and fine accessories. Stay at a high quality hotel. Use attractive graphics in your business presentations.

◘ The business world is very formal. Relationships become more casual only with time. Much attention is paid to status. Senior officials should always be addressed first.

◘ Use professional and courtesy titles (see their business cards). Ask before using first names, or wait until suggested by your host. In Mexico, Mr.=Senor,

Mrs. = Senora, Miss = Senorita, and the honorary title of "Don" may be used to show respect to older men or men of high social status, used with the first name only, e.g., Don Jose.

◘ Mexicans have two last names. For men and single women, use the first last name (father's family name), e.g., Jose Garcia Rodriguez would be addressed as Senor Garcia.

◘ Always take a period of time for small talk before getting down to business.

◘ There is a strong sense of pride. Loss of face in front of others is to be avoided. Conflict will be avoided, and it can be difficult to interpret negative reactions. For example, an answer of agreement may be given to show respect, when the actual answer is negative.

◘ Business negotiations are likely to start with generalities and lead to specifics slowly, in a style similar to that in the USA and Europe. (Haggling styles are found only in the open markets.) Building a "common culture" is suggested.

Body Language

◘ Physical embraces between men are common greetings.

◘ Handshakes should be firm and long, lasting about four or five shakes.

Asia

◘ Asian countries have a high group orientation, requiring consensus in all matters. There is no sense of "self" as the Western world defines it—people exist only as part of a family and other groups, not as individuals with rights. Conformity is valued over autonomy.

◘ There is strong respect for authority within the hierarchy to maintain harmony. As such, personal modesty is valued. The only "safe" humor is self-deprecatory.

◘ The Japanese have a seamless web of culture integrating business and government and social structure. There's no schism anywhere.

◘ More than anything else, Japanese fear mistakes and rejections, which would shame themselves as well as those they represent, e.g., their company and family.

◘ Asians consider persistence and hard work more important components of intelligence than cognitive ability.

◘ Asians never look back, only forward. Therefore, they don't go back to correct a mistake; rather, it is done again and again until perfection is attained. The focus is on the future.

◘ The Japanese believe good form is required to achieve the desired results. Such form is acquired through precise practice in skills such as martial arts, flower arranging, penmanship and even the art of initiating discussion. Thus, following procedures meticulously in business is also important.

◘ The Japanese deflect attention from their personal achievements, attributing their success to the support of their group. If complimented their response is likely to be, "No, no, it was nothing."

◘ Japanese subordinates are expected to meet performance expectations with little direction, encouragement or feedback from their supervisors, in keeping with the philosophies of Zen Buddhism. Positive feedback is considered unnecessary if you have performed well.

◘ Time is relative. Long-term relationships are paramount. To Americans, a five-year plan is "long." To Asians, a fifty-year plan is common.

◘ Clocks are inappropriate gifts in China as they may be interpreted as marking the passage of the recipient's life.

◘ The cow is sacred in India; therefore leather gifts are inadvisable.

◘ The number "5" is lucky in Asia, representing the five elements of earth, water, fire, sky and air.

- The Japanese think that to talk about culture and cross-cultural training means learning good manners in the other country.

- A respected intermediary is advisable in business meetings to help establish relationships with future business partners. Expect up to eight meetings before a decision can be reached in Japan.

- In Chinese, the surname comes first and the given name comes last, e.g., Mr. Lo Win Hao should be addressed as Mr. Lo.

- In China the phrase, "Have you eaten," is interpreted as inquiring about a person's health.

- A missing button, frayed cuff or cheap cuff links may be interpreted by the Japanese as a reflection of slovenly personal or work habits and a lack of dependability.

- Sensitivity to status is important in Japan. Always concentrate on dealing with the most senior man in the room, even if an interpreter is present.

- To avoid shame to anyone, and thus "save face," affirmative answers will be given to most questions. There are 16 different meanings to the word "yes" in Japanese. Confrontation will be avoided.

- The Japanese word "Hai" is a sign of acknowledgment, not necessarily agreement. This word is used in Japanese conversation frequently to let the speaker know that the listener is following the conversation, much as Americans may say, "Uh, Huh."

◘ With the Japanese, the more important the subject, the greater the need to be circumspect and avoid giving offense. Refusals may come in the form of, "It will be very difficult," "I will have to discuss it further," silence or unwarranted delays.

◘ Loud speech is regarded as lacking in refinement or threatening by the Japanese, who are encouraged not to dominate conversations or try to impress with words, and not to interrupt or speak over someone else.

◘ The Japanese regard hesitancy in answering an important question as a sign of maturity and giving due consideration to serious matters.

◘ Japanese insults are most often couched in vegetable metaphysical terms, e.g., an out-of-focus eggplant, or a terminal onion.

◘ When negotiating, allow silences. They can be meaningful and are common in Pacific Rim countries. Many Americans, uncomfortable with silence, have misinterpreted them and given away points prematurely.

◘ For the Japanese, the comment "By the way" is a signal to start talking about serious business matters.

◘ Whereas Japan used to emulate China, differences are evolving. While the Japanese avoid conflict, the Chinese now seem to like confrontation.

Body Language

◘ In Thailand the head is sacred and to touch it is offensive, even that of a child.

◘ Placing chopsticks upright in a bowl of rice signifies death.

◘ The handshake is likely to be a single firm gesture, accompanied with a bow. It is polite to return both.

◘ Do not use your left hand in India, or show the bottom of your shoe, such as sitting with crossed legs. Both are perceived as insults.

◘ In Malaysia, beckoning with the index finger to single out a person in a group is perceived as being treated like a child, and is insulting. In Indonesia, the gesture is used only to call animals. Pointing should be done with the thumb outward and the fingers closed in the palm.

◘ A smile may be used to hide embarassment or mask true feelings in Japan. In Korea smiling is reserved for intimate relationships. Broad smiles are considered inappropriate with strangers, and flirtatious for women.

◘ The Japanese are respectful of each other's personal space. Touching is inappropriate in most situations.

◘ Kissing is very private and never done in public.

◘ Broad sweeping gestures are impolite.

◘ A nod of the head means, "I hear you," not necessarily agreement.

◘ The Japanese usually bow when meeting others, using minimal facial expression. The depth, duration and repetition of the bow determines the communicator's social status, with the lower status being the greatest intensity.

◘ The Chinese greet a friend with a vigorous handshake and may put an arm around you.

Middle East

◘ Arabs have a high group orientation, tending to form into sub-groups which can be factionalistic.

◘ Time is elastic.

◘ Do not ask personal questions in the Middle East.

◘ Arabs hold hospitality, seniority and building relationships as top values.

Body Language

◘ The Arab handshake may be limp and lingering. Pulling the hand away too soon is interpreted as rejection.

INTERNATIONAL PHILOSOPHIES & PROTOCOL

◘ Eye contact must always be made in the Arab world when meeting another person because of the Arab belief that the eyes are the windows of the soul and to avert them is to expose their owner's lack of sincerity.

◘ Nodding your head up and down means "No."

◘ In Arab culture a common greeting among friends and acquaintances is a hug, although strangers usually greet with a handshake.

* * *

"What a future lies in store for the American, Japanese, German or Canadian youngster who works to become a global citizen. The opportunities in any direction you look—Canada, Mexico, Central and South America, Eastern and Western Europe, Asia—are matchless and unprecedented....I'm green with envy."

Tom Peters

CHAPTER 7

AFTERWORD

In reflecting on the foregoing sections, it seemed appropriate to revisit a couple of the author's earlier published essays, somewhat modified. The first addresses the human need to blame others for what happens to us; the second looks at the successes of transnational organizations. These articles address some of the human conditions we all have, and positive incentives to change.

OVERCOMING OUR NEED TO BLAME

Ever stub your toe and mumble, "Who put that there?" Or misplace a memo and think, "Who took my file?" You're not alone. Psychologists tell us that as soon as we realize there are aspects of ourselves we don't like, we externalize them onto others, creating a world of bad "them" vs. good "us." Consider the child who punches her doll after she trips and falls. Or as Howard Stein, editor of **The Journal of Psychoanalytic Anthropology** says in the August 28, 1989, issue of **Newsweek**, "We need the bad guys, the people who embody all that stuff we want to get rid of—our greed, anger, avarice." These tendencies can evolve into rival gangs on a school playground or rival enemies on a battlefield.

As is true with all things in nature, there is a closely-linked counterbalance to this negative need: the positive need for approval. When reprimanded by our supervisors, often we are tempted to pass that anger on to our subordinates, or blame someone else for our failure to meet the expectations of the "boss." In this world where 90 percent of the input we get is negative, what we really need is a word of praise or encouragement from our supervisors. When this happens often enough, and our personal needs for esteem are met, we naturally pass on the overflow of praise to others who have contributed to that positive performance, fulfilling their esteem needs. The end result is improved morale and increased productivity for everyone.

How can we get control of that negative side which wants to externalize our failings (real or perceived) onto others?

- Recognize these tendencies for what they are, and accept the fact that each of us is a flawed creature of nature—it is part of being human. Commit to controlling negative thoughts about ourselves or others.

- Learn to celebrate the uniqueness of each person, rather than trying to force others into the mold of our own preconceived perceptions. Resist judging others by our own values.

AFTERWORD

▸ Start with the common cords of humanity which bind us all together on this planet, and deal with differences as they arise. For example, when conversing with someone who is "different," search for a shared experience (such as waiting in line together, or both being a parent) which puts you both on equal footing and establishes a common base line from which to develop the relationship.

▸ In the workplace, create settings or environments where people can iron out their differences through discussion and mediation, if necessary, encouraging participants to see the other's point of view as well as their own.

It has been said that the hope of the future lies in the ability of adults to surrender their childhood need to blame.

* * *

UNITY FROM DIVERSITY

"How are we ever going to get everyone to pull together for the good of the company and value differences at the same time?" A valid question, and one asked by many sceptics of newer employee management philosophies. How, indeed, can we derive unity from diversity?

The answer can be summed up with the following diagram: **Diversity → Valued → Unity.™** Mitchell R. Hammer reports:

> "From the research perspective, I am encouraged by the recent and more empirically rigorous studies which suggest that a strong cultural/ethnic identity (ingroup identification) makes one feel more secure and therefore more open to outgroup members. Social identity theory also explains the mechanism in which new identities can emerge...The development of this kind of global identity represents an additional group identification; not a replacement of one's cultural ethnic group identity."

Applied to the workplace, when our uniqueness is respected, even celebrated, by the organizations where we work, we are much more motivated to contribute to the welfare of those organizations. In so doing we are not relinquishing our own cultural identity to that of the corporate culture; rather, we are creating additional dimensions to our individuality as members of a new group. Because we feel honored by that group, and thus a part of it, we take pride in its accomplishments and are more inclined to work for its success. That motivation increases as we share in its growth.

To demonstrate the dynamics of deriving unity from diversity, let's look at transnational organizations, where the differences among employees are even more pronounced than in America.

First, some definitions. Christopher A. Bartlett and Sumantra Ghoshal describe the "transnational" organization as one which integrates assets, resources and diverse people in operating units around the world. "Success in today's international climate...demands highly specialized yet closely linked groups of global business managers, country or regional managers, and worldwide functional managers." Traditional hierarchies do not have the flexibility this type of modern organization demands. Companies cited by the authors serve as case studies for successful development of global managers. Shared strategic capabilities are:

♦ Global-scale efficiency and competitiveness;

♦ National-level responsiveness and flexibility; and

♦ Cross-market capacity to leverage learning on a worldwide basis.

These capabilities reflect the extensive need for cross-cultural understanding.

In an earlier work Bartlett and Ghoshal recommended training program elements for global managers. Points emphasized were:

- Legitimizing diversity, maintaining a dynamic balance. Developing flexibility in problem-solving. Highlighting the advantages of incorporating the points of view of all cultures, not just emulating a pattern which has worked in the past but is based on obsolete hierarchical organizational structures. Managing complexity.

- Recognizing cultural differences and overcoming cultural barriers. Importance of pride of heritage in all cultures.

- Encouraging transnational innovations. Working together for mutual benefit—the inevitable give and take in such an environment.

- Importance of input (vs. imposition) of all facilities into the company's vision/mission statements. Insures that all affected operations' knowledge will be incorporated and guarantees buy-in of all parties. Result becomes a personal as well as a corporate goal.

- Creating an atmosphere where employees work as teams, share ideas and resources and have common values—where the people make it happen.

AFTERWORD

- Integrating local worldwide operations into a corporate network for new growth, development and worldwide competition.

- Identifying characteristics of transnational individuals and organizations, the lessons of history, management implications and challenges. The traditional vs. emerging change process models.

- Redefining the manager's role in a transnational context.

- Encouraging people who train together to build bonds and personal relationships—a network of informal contacts.

These concepts were corroborated at an executive conference I attended where the qualities of successful international managers were examined by representatives of Fortune 500 companies. In evaluating various factors, such as technical skills, success on the domestic front, personal motivation to take the international assignment, family situation and language skills, all agreed that the foremost success indicator was one called "Relational Dimensions." Aspects were:

- Tolerance for ambiguity

- Behavioral flexibility

- Nonjudgmentalism

- Cultural empathy

- Low ethnocentrism

- Interpersonal skills.

In other words, more than any other factor, the degree of success American managers had overseas correlated directly with their ability to relate to people in their new location. They needed the desire and ability to establish relationships with the local citizenry, building trust, and the flexibility to see situations through the eyes of other cultures.

Whether here or abroad we are living in a global economy, which is fast becoming a global workplace. How well we adapt to the human needs of the new marketplace will predict our success in the changing business environment. From these rich resources of diverse skills, talents and perspectives a world of new possibilities awaits us. Our challenge is to recognize and nurture those resources toward mutual prosperity.

* * *

AFTERW0RD

Aristotle once said, "An idiot is a person without a community."

In **The Moral Sense** James Q. Wilson provides scientific evidence suggesting that all peoples of the world are collective by nature—our DNA seeks it.

Even Alexis de Tocqueville, who stated that America promotes individualism, also noted that Americans are joiners, accommodating the human need to affiliate. As you may recall from Chapter 2, W. Hampton Sides concurs that Americans are joiners at heart.

In Wilson's book he proposes there are four universal moral senses in all humans:

Sympathy

Fairness

Self-Control

Duty

If he's right, and we can tap into these inherent qualities as we interact with our customers, colleagues and communities, we may well find the pathway to prosperity and peace for all.

* * *

"Our strength in this country is rooted in our diversity. Our history bears witness to that fact. E Pluribus Unum—it was a good idea when our country was founded, and it's a good idea today. From many, one. That still identifies us."

Barbara Jordan
U. S. Congress

Glossary

The following definitions are in common usage as of this writing and are those used in this book. It should be noted, however, that new meanings and interpretations evolve continually in this rapidly changing world.

African. Of or relating to the continent of Africa or its people. An inhabitant of Africa. A person of immediate or remote African ancestry, especially blacks.

African-American (also Afro-American). Of or relating to blacks living in the USA who also wish to be identified with their African ancestry. *(Editor's Note: Some blacks prefer to be identified with different home countries, e.g., Jamaica.)* An American of African and especially Negroid descent.

American. Of or relating to the United States of America (USA), its possessions or original territory. Also, of or relating to North America or South America, usually preceded by a qualifying adjective, such as "Latin" American. An inhabitant of the Americas. A citizen of the USA.

American Indian, Eskimo, and Aleut. A person having origins in any of the original peoples of North America, who maintains cultural identifications through tribal affiliation or community recognition. The term "American Indian" or abbreviation "AIEA" refers to the race group American Indian, Eskimo, and Aleut. (U.S. Census Bureau)

Anglo-American. Relating to cultural traditions which have evolved from early Northern European settlers of USA to present day. Views held by the current majority culture in USA. A person who follows these cultural values.

Asian and Pacific Islander. A person having origins in any of the original peoples of the Far East, Southeast Asia, the Indian subcontinent, or the Pacific Islands. This area includes, for example, China, India, Japan, Korea, the Philippine Islands, and Samoa. The term "Asian" or abbreviation "API" refers to the race group Asian and Pacific Islander. (U.S. Census Bureau) Category includes almost 70 countries incorporating considerable variety in customs and philosophies.

Black. A person having origins in any of the Black racial groups of Africa. (U.S. Census Bureau)

Caucasian. Of or relating to the white race of mankind as classified according to physical features, or as defined by law specifically as composed of persons of European, North African or southwest Asian ancestry.

Chicano/Chicana (male/female). Mexican American who is consciously and politically aware of the needs of the Mexican-American population.

Culture. The way of life of a society. The customs, ideas and attitudes shared by a group, which make up its culture, are transmitted from generation to generation by learning processes rather than biological inheritance. (New Columbia Encyclopedia)

Ethnic. Of or relating to large groups of people classed according to common racial, national, tribal, religious, linguistic, or cultural origin or background.

Hispanic. English word for a person of Mexican, Puerto Rican, Cuban, Central or South American or other Spanish culture or origin, regardless of race. (U.S. Census Bureau)

GLOSSARY

Latino/Latina (male/female). *Spanish word for Hispanic, usually preferred by those of Latin American descent.*

Minority. *Numerical term often used in reference to U.S. Census Bureau population classifications by race, i.e., any category less than the current majority population in the U.S.*

Native American. *A person born or raised in America. Also, term of preference by some American Indians, referring to indigenous ancestry.*

Race. *A division of mankind possessing traits that are transmissible by descent and sufficient to characterize it as a distinct human type. (Webster's)*

Race and Ethnic Definitions and Concepts: *The racial classification used by the U.S. Census Bureau generally adheres to the guidelines in Federal Statistical Directive No. 15, issued by the Office of Management and Budget, which provides standards on race and Hispanic-origin categories for statistical reporting to be used by all Federal agencies. (U.S. Census Bureau March 1994)*

White. *A person having origins in any of the original peoples of Europe, North Africa, or the Middle East. (U.S. Census Bureau)*

* * *

Selected References

Over 1,000 references were used in preparing this book. The following selections have been listed here because of their particular relevance to the foregoing chapters and potential applications for readers.

"A New Mix for America," **Chicago Tribune**, September 29, 1993.

"Advancing Women in the Workplace," **Training & Development**, September 1993.

"Afrocentrism," special report, **Newsweek**, September 23, 1991.

"America's Newest Immigrants Are Poorer - But Smarter," **Business Week**, October 11, 1993.

"American?," cover story on changes in American society, **Newsweek**, July 10, 1995.

"Americans Feel Families & Values Are Eroding But They Disagree Over the Causes and Solutions," **The Wall Street Journal**, June 11, 1993.

"Apprentice Program Develops Diverse Talent Pool," **HRMagazine**, April 1994.

"Asia 2000," Special report on Pacific Rim, **Fortune**, October 5, 1992.

"Asia's Wealth - It's Creating a Massive Shift in Global Economic Power," **Business Week**, November 29, 1993.

"Asking for Help: Why Men Can't," **Working Woman**, August 1992.

"Attention, Willard Scott: More and more people are living to see 100," **Newsweek**, May 4, 1992.

127

"Avoiding Sexual Stereotyping & Sexist Language," **BNAC Communicator**, Fall 1993.

"Big Hispanic Firms Have Brisk Sales Growth," **The Wall Street Journal**, July 8, 1992.

"Black Entrepreneurship," special section of **The Wall Street Journal**, April 3, 1992.

"Blacks on Blacks," **Fortune,** November 2, 1992.

"Brr-ring! America Calling - Deregulation hits European tellcom, and the U.S. comes running. Americans are all over the map," **Business Week**, June 1, 1992.

"Capitalizing on Global Diversity," **HRMagazine**, December 1992.

"China - Is Prosperity Creating a Freer Society?," **Business Week**, June 6, 1994.

"Computers - The Gender Divide," series in **The Wall Street Journal**, March 1994.

"Cracking the China Market," special section **The Wall Street Journal**, December 10, 1993.

"Cultural Diversity in Today's Corporation," special report in **Working Woman**, January 1991.

"Cultural Diversity Works, Study Says," **Training**, September 1993.

"Diverse Work Teams Matched or Outperformed Homogeneous Ones in U. of N. Texas Experiment," **The Wall Street Journal**, June 15, 1993.

"Diversity Programs Make Business Sense, Glass Ceiling Commission Official Says," **BNAC Communicator**, Spring/Summer 1994.

"Diversity Training Extends Beyond U.S.," **The Wall Street Journal**, March 12, 1993.

"Diversity Training - Hope, Faith & Cynicism," **Training**, January 1994.

"Dumber Than We Thought - Literacy: A New Study Shows Why We Can't Cope with Everyday Life," **Newsweek**, Sepgember 20, 1993.

"Employers Help Men Adapt to Changing Roles," **The Wall Street Journal**, July 28, 1992.

"Equal Opportunity Pays," **The Wall Street Journal**, May 4, 1993.

"Fitting Square Pegs Into Round Holes," **HRMagazine**, January 1994.

SELECTED REFERENCES

"German View - 'You Americans Work Too Hard - And for What?,'" **The Wall Street Journal**, July 14, 1994.

"Getting Older, Getting Better," **Training & Development Journal**, August 1990.

"Global Market, By Degrees - Americans Head to Europe for B-School," **Newsweek**, March 8, 1993.

"Going Global? Stifle Yourself!," **Training**, August 1995.

"Homophobia," **Newsweek**, February 14, 1994.

"How the Kims of Los Angeles and Other Koreans Made It in the U.S.," **The Wall Street Journal**, June 16, 1992.

"How the Men in Your Office Really See You (Interviews)," **Working Woman**, November 1991, pp. 101-103.

"Immigrant Impact Grows on U.S. Population," **The Wall Street Journal**, March 16, 1992.

"In Any Language, It's Unfair - More Immigrants Are Bringing Bias Charges Against Employers," **Business Week**, June 21, 1993.

"In Athens, It's Palms In," **Newsweek**, December 10, 1990.

"In Friends, Many See Reflection of Themselves," **The Wall Street Journal**, June 30, 1993.

"Innovation-The Global Race," special issue of **Business Week**, June 15, 1990.

"Inside the Black Business Network," **Business Week**, November 29, 1993.

"Integrating Steps for Bridging Race, Language, Gender Gaps, "**Training Directors Forum Newsletter**, Lakewood Publications, 1992.

"It's a Small (Business) World," special report on U.S. entrepreneurs going global, **Business Week**, April 17, 1995.

"Labor Pains - Re-examining the American Work Ethic," **Entrepreneur Magazine**, May 1994.

"Land of Opportunity - South Africa: American Blacks Look to Cash In," **Newsweek**, May 23, 1994.

"Latin America - The Big Move to Free Markets," **Business Week**, June 15, 1992.

"Men Who Work Together Stay Together," **Personnel Journal**, February 1992, p. 18.

"Minorities Gain Seats in Fortune 1,000," **The Wall Street Journal**, February 25, 1994.

"More Women Work, While Fewer Men Do," **The Wall Street Journal**, December 31, 1993.

"Motorola: Training for the Millenium," **Business Week**, March 28, 1994.

"Move Over, Boomers - The Busters Are Here - And They're Angry," **Business Week**, December 14, 1992.

"Ms. President - Other Nations Elect Women to Lead Them, So Why Doesn't U.S.?," **The Wall Street Journal**, December 14, 1993.

"Must Boys Always Be Boys?" (girls fighting sexual harassment at school), **Newsweek**, October 19, 1992.

"Myths & Facts About Older Women," National Commission on Working Women, **Working Age Newsletter**, May/June 1991.

"Office Woes East and West," **Fortune**, November 4, 1991, p. 14.

"Older Workers Are Good for Business," **Training & Development**, May 1994.

"Older Workers Increase Company Profits," **Personnel Journal**, December 1991, p. 8.

"One America - The North American free-trade pact may be just the first step toward a hemispheric bloc," special section of **The Wall Street Journal**, September 24, 1992.

"Real Men Buy Paper Towels, Too," **Business Week,** November 9, 1992.

"Record Number of EEOC Charges Filed in Fiscal Year 1993," **BNAC Communicator**, Spring/Summer 1994.

"Recruiting Minority Graduates," **Training & Development**, January 1994.

"Reinventing America - Meeting the New Challenges of a Global Economy," special issue of Business Week, published November 1, 1992. Includes "Paradigms for Postmodern Managers - The Accent Is on Adaptabiity" and "Diverse by Design - How Good Intentions Make Good Business."

"Smoothing Out Cultural Misunderstandings," **Training**, October 1992.

"Spanish Station Tops L.A. Radio Market," **The Wall Street Journal**, February 24, 1993.

SELECTED REFERENCES

"Talk About Your Dream Team - Can IBM, Siemens and Toshiba design the big chip? Maybe," **Business Week,** July 27, 1992.

"Teens - Here Comes the Biggest Wave Yet," **Business Week,** April 11, 1994.

"The 21st Century Family," Special Edition of **Newsweek,** Winter/Spring 1990.

"The Boomers Take Over in Japan," **Business Week,** October 25, 1993.

"The Building Blocks of the Learning Organization," **Training,** June 1994.

"The Crystal Ball Shows Asians & Hispanics Leading Worker Growth," **The Wall Street Journal,** January 4, 1994.

"The Effect of Cultural Differences on Japanese Managers & American Employees," **Training & Development,** April 1994.

"The Feminization of Leadership," **Training & Development,** February 1994.

"The Immigrants - How They're Helping the U.S. Economy," cover story of **Business Week,** July 13, 1992.

"The Invisible Diversity - Gays & Lesbians in Organizations," **Training & Development,** April 1993.

"The Mexican Worker - Smart, Motivated, Cheap - and a Potent New Economic Force to be Reckoned With," **Business Week,** April 19, 1993.

"The New Competitive Advantage -- Expanding the Participation of People with Disabilities in the American Work Force," special section of **Business Week,** May 30, 1994.

"The Past, Present & Future of Workplace Learning (special issue)," **Training & Development,** May 1994.

"The Science of Race," special issue of **Discover,** a monthly science magazine, November 1994.

"Think Globally, Sell Locally," **Training & Development,** December 1993.

"U.S. Companies Offer Diversity Training," **HRMagazine,** January 1994.

"U.S. Elderly Are Growing Steadily More Multiracial," **The Wall Street Journal,** February 3, 1993.

"U.S. Firms Face Costs of Cultural Chauvinism," **Orange County Register,** as reprinted in **Chicago Tribune,** April 17, 1995.

"Unlocking the Corporate Closet," **Training & Development**, January 1994.

"Welcome to the Real Melting Pot (Toronto, Canada)," **Business Week**, July 24, 1995

"What Kids Need To Know - Putting Cultural Literacy Into Elementary School," **Newsweek**, November 2, 1992.

"When Johnny Comes Marching Home Again...influx will help plug skills gap," **Industry Week**, August 17, 1992.

"When Worlds Collide - How Columbus's Voyages Transformed Both East and West," special issue of **Newsweek**, Fall/Winter 1991.

"White, Male and Worried," **Business Week**, January 31, 1994.

"Why Baby Busters Aren't Going Bust," **Working Woman**, April 1994.

"Widespread Sexual Bias Found in Courts," **The Wall Street Journal**, August 20, 1992.

"Willing and Able: Americans with Disabilities in the New Work Force," special section in **Business Week**, October 28, 1991.

"Women in Business: A Global Report Card," **The Wall Street Journal**, July 26, 1995.

"Women, Minorities Own More Small Businesses," **The Wall Street Journal**, August 12, 1992.

"Work and Family - Companies Are Starting to Respond to Workers' Needs - and Gain From It," **Business Week,** June 28, 1993.

"Work Teams Demonstrate Diverse Advantages," **Training & Development**, October 1993.

"Working Women Adding to Their Numbers," **The Wall Street Journal**, March 10, 1995.

"World Business - The Emerging Boom," special section **The Wall Street Journal,** September 24, 1993.

"Young Adults Point Up Growing U.S. Diversity," **The Wall Street Journal**, December 7, 1992.

SELECTED REFERENCES

Adler, Nancy J., "Women Managers in a Global Economy," **Training & Development**, April 1994.

Ali, Ellen Boyer, "Check Your Gender Bias," **Training & Development**, April 1994.

Altany, David R., "If Women Ran Industry," **Industry Week**, September 20, 1993.

Alter, Jonathan, "The Cultural Elite," cover story in **Newsweek**, October 5, 1992.

Althen, Gary, **American Ways - A Guide for Foreigners in the United States**, Intercultural Press, Inc., Yarmouth, Maine 1988.

Anders, George, "NIH (National Institutes of Health) Pushes for Diversity in Research," **The Wall Street Journal**, March 8, 1994.

Arzac, Adriana, "Living Intercultural Legends - Edward C. Stewart," **Communique**, February/March 1991, SIETAR, New York, NY.

Asbell, Bernard, **What They Know About You**, Random House, 1991.

Axtell, Roger, E., **Do's and Taboos Around the World - A Guide to International Behavior**, The Benjamin Company, Inc., Elmsford, NY, 1985.

Ball, Chuck, "A White Man's Journey," **The Diversity Factor**, Spring 1993.

Barker, Joel Arthur, **Discovering the Future - The Business of Paradigms**, ILI Press, St. Paul, MN, 1985.

Barnet, Richard J., & Cavanagh, John, **Global Dreams: Imperial Corporations & the New World Order**, Simon & Schuster, NY, 1994.

Barrentine, Pat, **When the Canary Stops Singing: Women's Perspectives on Transforming Business,** Berrett-Koehler Publishers, San Francisco, 1994.

Barrett, Paul M., "Justices Make It Easier to Prove Sexual Harassment," **The Wall Street Journal**, November 10, 1993.

Barrett, Paul M., "More Minorities, Women Named to U.S. Courts," **The Wall Street Journal**, December 23, 1993.

Bartlett, Christopher A., and Ghoshal, Sumantra, "What Is a Global Manager?," **Harvard Business Review**, September-October 1992.

Bartlett, Christopher A., and Ghoshal, Sumantra, **Managing Across Borders: The Transnational Solution**, Harvard Business School Press, Cambridge, MA, 1989.

Beck, Melinda, "The New Middle Age," **Newsweek**, December 7, 1992.

Begley, Sharon, "Gray Matters," **Newsweek**, March 27, 1995.

Berger, Michael, "Building Bridges Over the Cultural Rivers," **International Management,** Vol. 42, No. 7/8, July/August 1987, pp. 61-62.

Best, William J., "Training Japanese Leaders for Western Firms," **The Wall Street Journal**, May 11, 1992.

Bly, Robert, **Iron John: A Book About Men,** Addison-Wesley Publishing Company, Reading, MA, 1990.

Bolton, Robert, PhD, **People Skills**, Simon & Schuster, 1979.

Boorstein, Daniel J., "I Am Optimistic - Pulitzer Prize Winning Historian on America's Future," **Parade**, July 10, 1994.

Bowers, Brent, "Tapping Foreign Talent Pool Can Yield Lush Growth," **The Wall Street Journal**, March 23, 1992.

Braganti, Nancy L., and Devine, Elizabeth, **European Customs & Manners**, Simon and Schuster, New York, NY, 1984.

Braham, Jim, "No, You Don't Manage Everyone the Same," **Industry Week**, February 6, 1989, pp. 28-35.

Bravo, Ellen, and Cassedy, Ellen, **The 9 to 5 Guide to Combatting Sexual Harassment,** Wiley & Sons, 1992.

Bredin, James, "Inside INSEAD - Multiculturalism is Basic at Europe's Best B-School," **Industry Week**, July 20, 1992.

Brown, Thomas L., "Women in Business: New Thinking?," **Industry Week**, February 3, 1992, p. 22.

Brown, Tom, "Joel Barker - New Thoughts on Paradigms," **Industry Week**, May 18, 1992.

Brown, Tom, "Richard Pascale: The 'Christopher Columbus' of Management?," **Industry Week**, January 7, 1991, pp. 12-20.

Byrne, John A., "Wharton Rewrites the Book on B-Schools," **Business Week**, May 13, 1991, p. 43.

Candron, Shari, "Surviving Cross-Cultural Shock," **Industry Week**, July 6, 1992.

SELECTED REFERENCES

Carey, Patricia M., "Bank On It (African Americans Pictured on Bank Checks)," **Your Company**, Fall 1993.

Chen, Chris, "The Diversity Paradox," **Personnel Journal**, January 1992, pp. 32-36.

Cheslow, Jerry, "Selling Your Services Overseas," **Home Office Computing**, July 1991.

Choo, Ai Leng, "Asian-Americans' Political Clout Grows as Candidates Target Them for Funding," **The Wall Street Journal**, February 21, 1992.

Chu, Chin-Ning, **The Asian Mind Game**, Macmillan Publishing Co, New York, 1991.

Cook, Brian M., "Global Competition - The European Way," **Industry Week**, July 6, 1992.

Coontz, Stephanie, **The Way We Never Were: American Families and the Nostalgia Trap,** Harper-Collins Publishers, 1992.

Copeland, Lennie, & Griggs, Lewis, **Going International - How to Make Friends and Deal Effectively in the Global Marketplace,** Random House, New York, NY, 1985.

Cose, Ellis, "Black Men & Black Women," **Newsweek**, June 5, 1995.

Cose, Ellis, "Breaking the 'Code of Silence' - Black Leaders Face Up to Violent Crime," **Newsweek**, January 10, 1994.

Crawford, Susan, "A Brief History of Sexual-Harassment Law," **Training**, August 1994.

Cultural Diversity at Work, Bi-monthly Newsletter, The GilDeane Group, 13751 Lake City Way N.E., Suite 106, Seattle, WA 98125-3615.

Curran, John J., "China's Investment Boom," **Fortune**, March 7, 1994.

D'Amico, Esther, "Multicultural Marketing," **Home Office Computing**, August 1994.

DeGeorge, Gail, "Latin America's Newest Capitol City: Miami," **Business Week**, September 30, 1991, pp. 120-122.

Deutschman, Alan, "What 25-Year-Old's Want," **Fortune**, August 27, 1990, pp. 42-50.

Dovidio, John, "The Subtlety of Racism," **Training & Development**, April 1993.

Dreyfuss, Joel, "Get Ready for the New Work Force," **Fortune**, April 23, 1990.

Early, Gerald, **Lure and Loathing: Essays on Race, Identity, and the Ambivalence of Assimilation (Essays by Black Intellectuals)**, Allen Lane/Penguin Books, 1993.

Eiben, Therese, "U.S. Exporters on a Global Roll," **Fortune**, June 29, 1992.

Ellis IV, John W., "Communicating Between Cultures," **Crain's Chicago Business**, August 8, 1994.

Evans, David L., "The Wrong Examples (of Black Males)," **Newsweek**, March 1, 1993.

Evans, Sybil, "Resolving Conflicts with Diverse Groups - A Key Management Skill," **BNAC Communicator**, Spring/Summer 1993.

Evans, Sybil, "The Men's Forum at DuPont," **Cultural Diversity at Work**, July 1995.

Farney, Dennis, "National Paradox: As America Triumphs, Americans Are Awash In Doubt, Pessimism. Too Much Individualism?," **The Wall Street Journal**, July 27, 1992.

Fierman, Jaclyn, "Is Immigration Hurting the U.S.? No - Newcomers Create Far More Wealth Than They Consume," **Fortune**, August 9, 1993.

Filipczak, Bob, "Is It Getting Chilly in Here? Men & Women at Work," **Training**, February 1994.

Filipczak, Bob, "It's Just a Job - Generation X at Work," **Training**, April 1994.

Flaherty, Roger, "Hispanics Most Likely to Stay and Graduate, Studies at UIC Show," **Chicago Sun-Times**, November 23, 1990.

Fried, N. Elizabeth, **Sex, Laws & Stereotypes**, SHRM (Society for Human Resource Management), 1994.

Fyock, Catherine D., **America's Work Force Is Coming of Age**, Lexington Books, 1990.

Gaiter, Dorothy J., "The Gender Divide: Black Women's Gains in Corporate America Outshine Black Men's," **The Wall Street Journal**, March 8, 1994.

Gaiter, Dorothy, J., "A Black Entrepreneur Vaults Racial Barriers in a Southern Town," **The Wall Street Journal**, April 29, 1992.

Galagan, Patricia A., "Navigating the Differences," **Training & Development**, April 1993.

Gardenswartz, Lee, and Rowe, Anita, "How To Make Meeting Work in a Culturally Diverse Group," **Working World**, 1992.

Gates, Jr., Henry Louis, **Colored People**, Knopf, NY, 1994.

SELECTED REFERENCES

Geber, Beverly, "The Challenge of Multilingual Meetings," **Off-Site Meetings**, Lakewood Publications, July 1994.

Geber, Beverly, "The Care and Breeding of Global Managers," **Training**, July 1992.

Geber, Beverly, "The Disabled: Ready, Willing and Able," **Training**, December 1990, pp.29-36.

Gelman, David, "Why We All Love to Hate," **Newsweek**, August 28, 1989, pp. 62-64.

Gerein, Andrea, "Radio Stations Gain by Going After Hispanics," **The Wall Street Journal**, July 14, 1993.

Giles, Jeff, "Generation X - The Images Baby Boomers Have of 20-somethings Are Mostly Unfair and Untrue," **Newsweek**, June 6, 1994.

Gilsdorf, J.W., "The New Generation: Older Workers," **Training and Development**, March 1992, pp. 77-80.

Goodman, David, "Men Like Wives' Earnings But Are Mixed On Careers," **Chicago Tribune**, August 27, 1995.

Goozner, Merrill, "Japan Attempts Less-Rigid Schooling," **Chicago Tribune**, August 28, 1995.

Gordon, Jack, "The Team Troubles That Won't Go Away (Pitfalls of Hierarchies and Teams)," **Training**, August 1994.

Gorman, Christine, "How Gender May Bend Your Thinking," **Time**, July 17, 1995.

Graham, Ellen, "Schools Try Lessons in Tolerance to Battle Bias," **The Wall Street Journal**, April 10, 1995.

Gray, John, **Men Are From Mars, Women Are From Venus**, HarperCollins, NY, 1992.

Grossman, Laurie M., "After Demographic Shift, Atlanta Mall Restyles Itself As Black Shopping Center," **The Wall Street Journal**, February 26, 1992.

Hagerty, Bob, "Training Helps Expatriate Employees Build Bridges to Different Cultures," **The Wall Street Journal**, June 14, 1993.

Hall, Edward T., **Beyond Culture**, Anchor Press/Doubleday, New York, 1977.

Hall, Edward T., **The Basic Works of Edward T. Hall**, Anchor/Doubleday, New York, NY.

Hampden-Turner, Charles, & Trompenaars, Alfons, **The Seven Cultures of Capitalism - Value Systems for Creating Wealth in the United States, Japan, Germany, France, Britain, Sweden and the Netherlands**, Currency-Doubleday, NY, 1994.

Harris, Philip R.; Moran, Robert T., **Managing Cultural Differences**, Third Edition, Gulf Publishing Company, Houston, 1991.

Hart, Maria, "Taking a Chance - Elizabeth Sung tries a new path with 'Y & R' role," **Chicago Tribune**, June 30, 1994.

Haskell, Molly, "Managing Your Sexuality," **Working Woman,** August 1994.

Hayflick, P. Faith, and Lomperis, Anne E., "Why Don't They Speak English?," **Training,** October 1992.

Helgesen, Sally, **The Female Advantage**, Doubleday, 1990.

Henry III, William A. Henry, "Beyond the Melting Pot," **Time Magazine**, April 9, 1990, pp. 28-35.

Hill, Linda A., "Hardest Lessons for First-Time Managers - Paradoxically, To Treat People Fairly Is To Treat Them Differently," **Working Woman**, February 1994.

Hirsch, James S; Alexander, Suzanne; "Middle-Class Blacks Quit Northern Cities and Settle in the South," **The Wall Street Journal**, May 22, 1990.

Hofstede, Geert, **Cultures and Organizations**, McGraw-Hill, New York, 1991.

Hudy, John J., Warren, Ronald A., & Guest, Christopher W., "The Case for 'Personality Tests' in Training," **Training,** December 1991.

Huey, John, "Finding New Heroes for a New Era," **Fortune**, January 25, 1993.

Hwang, Suein L., "From Choices to Checkout, the Genders Behave Very Differently in Supermarkets," **The Wall Street Journal**, March 22, 1994.

Hyatt, Joshua, "The Partnership Route (It's possible to crack a foreign market on your own, but you may live to regret it.)," **Inc. Magazine**, December 1988.

Imai, Masaaki, **Never Take Yes For An Answer - An Inside Look At Japanese Business for Foreign Businessmen**, The Simul Press, Tokyo, Japan, 1975.

Ingrassia, Lawrence, "Gay, Lesbian Groups Seek to Expunge Bias They See in Language," **The Wall Street Journal**, May 3, 1993.

SELECTED REFERENCES

Intercultural Press, Inc., P. O. Box 700, Yarmouth, Maine 04096, a variety of publications.

International Business Magazine, monthly, 500 Mamaroneck Avenue, Harrison, NY 10528.

International Journal of Intercultural Relations, Pergamon Press, 660 White Plains Road, Tarrytown, NY 10591-5153.

Jacob, Rahul, "India Is Opening for Business," **Fortune**, November 16, 1992.

Jacob, Rahul, "Overseas Indians Make It Big - Richest Foreign-Born Group in U.S.," **Fortune**, November 15, 1993.

Jacob, Rahul, "The Big Rise - Middle Classes Explode Around Globe, Bringing New Markets & New Prosperity," **Fortune**, May 30, 1993.

Jamieson, David; O'Mara, Julie, **Managing Workforce 2000 - Gaining the Diversity Advantage**, Jossey-Bass Inc., San Francisco, CA, 1991.

Kang, Grace, "Asian-Americans Surge Into Legal Ranks," **The Wall Street Journal**, July 29, 1992.

Kantrowitz, Barbara, "Men, Women & Computers," **Newsweek**, May 16, 1994.

Kato, Hiroko, and Stern, Joan, **Understanding and Working with the Japanese Business World**, Prentice Hall, New York, 1992.

Kennedy, Jim, and Everest, Anna, "Put Diversity in Context: Your Company's Success May Depend on Its Ability to Compete for Tomorrow's Multicultural Work Force. Communication Is Key.," **Personnel Journal**, September 1991, pp. 50-54.

Kiester Jr., Edwin, "'Germany Prepares Kids for Good Jobs; We Were Preparing Ours for Wendy's,'" **Smithsonian**, March 1993.

King, Thomas, **Green Grass, Running Water (American Indian)**, Houghton Mifflin, 1993.

Kirkland, Jr., Richard I., "Why We Will Live Longer...And What It Will Mean," **Fortune**, February 21, 1994.

Kleiman, Carol, "Understanding cultures broadens horizons," **Chicago Tribune**, October 19, 1994.

Kochman, Thomas, **Black and White Styles in Conflict**, University of Chicago Press 1981. (University of Illinois communications professor explores communication styles of diverse students)

Korn/Ferry International, Andersen Graduate School of Management, **Decade of the Executive Woman**, Korn/Ferry International, 1993.

Kotkin, Joel, **Tribes**, Random House 1992. (How race, religion and identity determine success in the new global economy.)

Kotlowitz, Alex, and Alexander, Suzanne, "Tacit Code of Silence on Matters of Race Perpetuates Divisions - Blacks Reluctant to Share Experiences; Whites Shun Topic," **The Wall Street Journal**, May 28, 1992.

Kotulak, Ronald, "Unlocking the Mind," **Chicago Tribune**, September 21, 1994.

Kraar, Louis, "Korea Goes for Quality," **Fortune**, April 18, 1994.

Kroll, Jack, "Mambo King of Comedy - A Sensational One-Man Panorama of Hispanic Life," **Newsweek**, December 14, 1992.

Laabs, Jennifer J., "Corporate Anthropologists," **Personnel Journal**, January 1992, pp. 81-91.

Labick, Kenneth, "Class in America - Old Socioeconomic Rankings Changing," **Fortune**, February 7, 1994.

Lawrence-Lightfoot, Sara, **I've Known Rivers**, Addison-Wesley 1994. (Harvard Professor writes about middle-class African-Americans.)

Lee, Melissa, "Diversity Training Brings Unity to Small Companies," **Wall Street Journal**, September 2, 1993.

Lees, Gene, **Cats of Any Color, Jazz Black and White**, Oxford University Press 1994. (Essays by diverse jazz artists)

Lemonick, Michael D., "Glimpses of the Mind," cover story in **Time**, July 17, 1995.

Lewin, Roger, **The Origin of Modern Humans**, Scientific American Library, 1993.

Loden, Marilyn, and Rosener, Judy B., **Workforce America: Managing Employee Diversity as a Vital Resource**, American Society of Training and Development, Alexandria, VA, 1991.

Lopez, Gerald P., "We Should Be Counted - Latinos are routinely left off lists of America's influential peple," **Newsweek**, November 2, 1992.

SELECTED REFERENCES

Lopez, Juli Amparano, "Firms Elevate Heads of Diversity Programs," **The Wall Street Journal**, August 5, 1992.

Lord, Bette Bao, "Walking in Lucky Shoes - America is a road cleared by the footfalls of millions of immigrants," **Newsweek**, July 6, 1992. Lord, author of **Legacies: A Chinese Mosaic**, returned to China in 1989 as the wife of the American ambassador.

Lublin, Joann S., "Companies Use Cross-Cultural Training to Help Their Employees Adjust Abroad," **The Wall Street Journal**, August 4, 1992.

Lublin, Joann S., "Spouses Find Themselves Worlds Apart As Global Commuter Marriages Increase," **The Wall Street Journal**, August 19, 1992.

Lublin, Joann S., "Husbands in Limbo - As More Men Become 'Trailing Spouses,' Firms Help Them Cope," **The Wall Street Journal**, April 13, 1993.

Lubman, Sarah, "More Schools Embrace 'Full Inclusion' of the Disabled," **The Wall Street Journal**, April 13, 1994.

Magnusson, Paul, "With Latin America Thriving, NAFTA Might Keep Marching South," **Business Week**, July 25, 1994.

Managing Diversity, Monthly Newsletter, JALMC, P. O. Box 819, Jamestown, NY, 14702-0819.

Marsh, Barbara, "Gender Gap - Businesswomen Face Formidable Barriers When They Venture Overseas," **The Wall Street Journal**, October 16, 1992.

Marsh, Barbara "Market Booms for Multicultural Educational Products," **The Wall Street Journal**, March 24, 1993.

Marshall, Ray, and Tucker, Marc, **Thinking for a Living - Education and the Wealth of Nations,** Basic Books, 1992.

Martin, Judith, "Simple Greeting Becomes a Race Issue," **Chicago Tribune**, July 22, 1995.

Martin, Tom, "The World Economy - There's New Life in the Global Economy, And It's Going to Get Better," **Fortune**, July 25, 1994.

Mathews, Tom; Underwood, Anne; "America's Changing Face," **Newsweek**, September 10, 1990.

McAllister, Kim, "The X Generation," **HRMagazine**, May 1994.

McCarthy, Michael J., "Why German Firms Choose Carolina's to Build U.S. Plants," **The Wall Street Journal**, May 4, 1993.

McClenahen, John S., "North America's New Shape," **Industry Week**, September 21, 1992.

McClenahen, John S., "Title Slight (in Europe) Can Be Dangerous," **Industry Week**, April 20, 1992.

McCracken, David, "Study (on education) looks at role of cultural expectations," **Chicago Tribune**, April 4, 1993.

McKenna, Joseph F., "High-Performance Blueprint - Business and industry have to be part of the plan to upgrade schools and the workforce, says a blue-ribbon commission," **Industry Week**, June 1, 1992.

Mehta, Stephanie N., "New Magazines Target U.S.-Born Ethnic Minorities," **The Wall Street Journal**, July 26, 1994.

Menchu, Rigoberta, **I, Rigoberta Menchu: An Indian Woman in Guatemala**, Routledge, Chapman & Hall, 1985. 1992 Nobel Prize winner as "symbol of peace and reconciliation across ethnic, cultural and social dividing lines" in Guatemala and abroad.

Miller, Annetta, "The World 'S' Ours: From Spain to Singapore, Toys 'R' Us Expands Its Empire Overseas," **Newsweek**, March 23, 1992.

Miller, Karen Lowry, "And You Thought Japan Couldn't Learn from Detroit," **Business Week**, November 2, 1992.

Milwid, Beth, **Working with Men**, Beyond Words Publishing, 1990.

Monthly Labor Review, November 1991, articles on the outlook to 2005 for the economy, the labor force and employment, U.S. Department of Labor, Bureau of Labor Statistics, Washington, D.C. 20402.

Moran, Robert T., **Cultural Guide to Doing Business in Europe**, Stoneham, MA: Butterworth-Heinemann, 1992.

Morical, Keith, and Tsai, Benhong, "Adapting Training for Other Cultures," **Training and Development**, April 1992.

Morrison, Toni, Black novelist who challenges the roles of language, race and gender. Writings include: **Jazz** (Knopf), New York Times best-seller; **Playing in the Dark: Whiteness and the Literary Imagination** (Harvard University Press); **Beloved** (Knopf), winner of 1988 Pulitzer Prize.

SELECTED REFERENCES

Moskal, Brian S., "The Return of a Native - Zebra Technologies transfers manufacturing back from Japan with results of higher quality and lower cost," **Industry Week**, July 6, 1992.

Moynahan, Brigid, "Creating Harassment-Free Work Zones," **Training & Development**, May 1993.

Murphy, Terence, "Boomers, Busters and 50-Plussers: Managing the New Generation Gaps," **Working Woman**, July 1991.

National Public Radio (NPR) and Public Television, various programs such as NPR's daily "Morning Edition" and "All Things Considered" and special programs such as "The Great Divide and Affirmative Action in America," "Race Relations in the United States," and "Men's Roles." Among public television's offerings are the 10-hour series "Milennium" on America's diversity of values, beliefs, cultures, places and generations.

Nerburn, Kent, and Mengelkoch, Louise, **Native American Wisdom**, New World Library, San Rafael, CA, 1991.

O'Brien, Kathleen, "Grooming Women for the Top," **Working Woman**, July 1994.

O'Brien, Patricia, "Why Men Don't Listen," **Working Woman**, February 1993.

O'Malley, Kathy, "Guide for a Family Man," **Chicago Tribune**, August 6, 1995.

O'Reilly, Brian, "Reengineering the MBA - Quant Jocks Could Be Out, Verbal Types In," **Fortune**, January 24, 1994.

O'Reilly, Brian, "Your New Global Work Force," **Fortune**, December 14, 1992.

Okri, Ben, **Songs of Enchantment (Parable of Nation Building in Modern Nigeria)**, Doubleday, 1993.

Orenstein, Peggy, **SchoolGirls - Young Women, Self-Esteem, and the Confidence Gap**, Doubleday 1994.

Overman, Stephanie, "Good Faith Is the Answer - Accommodating Religion in the Workplace," **HRMagazine**, January 1994.

Overman, Stephanie, "Heroes for Hire - Hiring the Ex-Military," **HRMagazine**, December 1993.

Overman, Stephanie, "Temporary Services Go Global," **HRMagazine**, August 1993.

Overman, Stephanie, "You Don't Have to Be a Big Fish to Swim in International Waters," **HRMagazine**, September 1993.

Pease, Allan, **Signals**, Bantam Books, 1984.

Pedersen, Paul, "Mediating Multicultural Conflict by Separating Behaviors from Expectations in a Cultural Grid," **International Journal of Intercultural Relations**, Vol. 17, Pergamon Press Ltd., 1993.

Pennar, Karen, "The Global Economy Needs Bridges - Not Walls," **Business Week**, August 12, 1993.

Peters, Tom, "Why Americans Don't Succeed Overseas: We Can't See Beyond Our Borders," **Chicago Tribune**, June 15, 1992.

Petrini, Catherine M., "The Language of Diversity," **Training & Development**, April 1993.

Randlesome, Collin, **Business Cultures in Europe**, Stoneham, MA: Butterworth-Heinemann, 1992.

Rapoport, Carla, "The New U.S. Push Into Europe," **Fortune**, January 10, 1994.

Reading Across Boundaries, International Orientation Resources, 500 Skokie Blvd., Northbrook, IL 60062.

Rearwin, David, **The Asia Business Book**, Intercultural Press, Yarmouth, Maine, 1991.

Reitman, Valerie, "To Succeed in Russia, U.S. Retailer Employs Patience and Local Ally," **The Wall Street Journal**, May 27, 1993.

Reitman, Valerie, "Tots Do Swimmingly in Language-Immersion Programs," **The Wall Street Journal**, February 15, 1994.

Reynolds, David S., **Walt Whitman's America: A Cultural Biography**, Knopf 1995.

Rhinesmith, Stephen H., "Open the Door to a Global Mindset," **Training & Development**, May 1995.

Rhinesmith, Stephen H., "Global Mindsets for Global Managers," **Training & Development**, October 1992.

Rice, Faye, "How to Make Diversity Pay," **Fortune**, August 8, 1994.

Richman, Louis S., "Global Growth Is on a Tear," **Fortune**, March 20, 1995.

Rowland, Diana, **Japanese Business Etiquette**, Warner Books, New York, NY, 1985.

Rubin, Barry Louis, "Europeans Value Diversity," **HRMagazine**, January 1991.

SELECTED REFERENCES

Rubin, Don, "Cultural Bias Undermines Assessment," **Personnel Journal**, May 1992.

Sadken, Myra & David, **Failing at Fairness: How America's Schools Cheat Girls**, Scribners, 1994.

Samovar, Larry; Porter, Richard E., **Intercultural Communication: A Reader**, 7th Edition, and **Communication Between Cultures**, Wadsworth Publishing Company, Belmont, CA, 1994.

Sandberg, Jared, "People Are Hugging a Lot More Now & Seem to Like It," **The Wall Street Journal,** March 15, 1993.

Scheele, Adele, "Coping with Ageism," **Working Woman**, February 1994.

Scheele, Adele, "Learning to Compete with Women," **Working Woman,** November 1992.

Schein, Edgar H., "How Can Organizations Learn Faster? The Challenge of the Green Room," **Sloan Management Review**, Massachusetts Institute of Technology, Fall 1990, Vol. 32, No. 1, Boston Mass.

Schlender, Brenton R., "The Values We Will Need," **Fortune**, January 27, 1992.

Schwartz, Felice A., **Breaking with Tradition - Women and Work, the New Facts of Life**, Warner Books, 1992.

Seligman, Daniel, "The Case for White Males," **Fortune**, January 28, 1991, p. 107.

Seligson, Susan V., "What Women Do Better," **Redbook**, August 1993.

Senge, Peter M., **The Fifth Discipline**, Doubleday, New YOrk 1990.

Sheehy, Gail, **New Passages**, Random House, 1995.

Shorris, Earl, **Latinos - A Biography of the People**, W.W. Norton Company 1992.

Sides, W. Hampton, **Stomping Grounds: A Pilgrim's Progress Through Eight American Subcultures**, Morrow 1992.

Simons, George F., and Weissman, G. Deborah, **Men and Women: Partners At Work**, Crisp Publications, Los Altos, CA, 1990.

Simurda, Stephen J., "When Foreign Owners Boost a Sagging Industry," **International Business**, April 1992.

Smith, Mary Ann; Johnson, Sandra J., **Valuing Differences in the Workplace**, American Society of Training and Development, Alexandria, VA, 1991.

Soloman, Julie, "As Cultural Diversity Grows, Experts Urge Appreciation of Differences," **The Wall Street Journal**, September 12, 1990.

Soloman, Julie, "Firms Address Workers' Cultural Variety," **The Wall Street Journal**, February 10, 1989.

Solomon, Charlene Marmer, "Keeping Hate Out of the Workplace," **Personnel Journal,** July 1992.

Solomon, Charlene Marmer, "Managing the Baby Busters," **Personnel Journal**, March 1992.

Stern, Paul, "Free Trade with Mexico, Jobs for Americans," **The Wall Street Journal,** July 14, 1992.

Stewart, Edward C., and Bennett, Milton J., **American Cultural Patterns: A Cross-Cultural Perspective**, Revised Edition, Intercultural Press, Yarmouth, ME, 1991.

Storti, Craig, **The Art of Crossing Cultures**, Intercultural Press, Yarmouth ME, 1990.

Tannen, Deborah, **You Just Don't Understand - Women and Men in Conversation,** Ballantine Books, New York, 1991.

Tannenbaum, Jeffrey A., "Black Entrepreneur Specially Tailors Toys for Minorities," **The Wall Street Journal**, December 2, 1993.

Teodorescu, Gabriela, "Service With a Smile...in Russia?," **The Wall Street Journal**, August 16, 1995.

The Dictionary of Cultural Literacy, Houghton Mifflin Co., 1994.

The Diversity Factor, quarterly publication, Elsie Y. Cross Associates, Inc., P.O. Box 3188, Teaneck, NJ 07666.

The Diversity Training Bulletin, The GilDeane Group, Seattle, WA 1993.

The New Columbia Encyclopedia, Edited by William H. Harris and Judith S. Levey, Columbia University Press, 1975.

Thiederman, Sondra, **Bridging Cultural Barriers for Corporate Success**, Lexington Books, 1991.

SELECTED REFERENCES

Thomas, Jr., R. Roosevelt, **Beyond Race and Gender; Unleashing the Power of Your Total Work Force by Managing Diversity,** AMACOM, New York, 1991.

Trice, Harrison M., & Beyer, Janice M., **The Cultures of Work Organizations,** Prentice-Hall, 1993.

Turecamo, Dorrine, "Small Talk Is a Big Thing," **HRMagazine,** March 1994.

Utroska, Donald R., "Doing Business Abroad," **HRMagazine,** January 1993.

Wagner, Ellen J., **Sexual Harassment in the Workplace,** AMACOM, New York, NY 1992.

Waters, Harry F., "Listening to the Latin Beat - TV Networks Court the Hispanic Market," **Newsweek,** March 28, 1994.

Waters, Jr., Harry, "Preparing the African-American Student for Corporate Success: A Focus on Cooperative Education," **International Journal of Intercultural Relations,** Vol 14, pp. 365-376, 1990.

Webb, Susan L., **Step Forward - Sexual Harassment in the Workplace,** MasterMedia Ltd., 1991.

Webster's Ninth New Collegiate Dictionary, Merriam-Webster Inc., Springfield, MA, 1991.

Webster's Third New International Dictionary of the English Language Unabridged, G. & C. Merriam Company, Springfield, MA, 1971.

Westendorf, Sara, "Getting the Guys on Your Side," **Working Woman,** July 1993.

Wilkinson, Endymion, **Misunderstanding - Europe vs. Japan,** Chuokoron-sha, Inc., Tokyo, Japan, 1981.

Williams, Jerry L., "Latinos Love Training," **Training & Development,** March 1994.

Wilson, James Q., **The Moral Sense,** The Free Press (Macmillan), 1993. (Professor at UCLA explores social inclinations in scientific context.)

Wilson, Leland (Editor), **The Will Rogers Touch,** Brethren Press, Elgin, IL, 1978.

Woodward, Kenneth L., "The (Religious) Rites of Americans," **Newsweek,** November 29, 1993.

Workforce 2000, Hudson Institute and U. S. Department of Labor, 1987, update report by Hudson Institute and Towers Perrin, 1990.

MULTICULTURAL COMMUNICATION STRATEGIES

Workforce Diversity, Monthly Newsletter, Remy Publishing Company, 350 West Hubbard Street, Suite 440, Chicago, IL 60610.

Wynter, Leon E., "Minorities Play the Hero in More TV ADs as Clients Discover Multicultural Sells," **Wall Street Journal**, November 24, 1993.

Wynter, Leon E., "Trying to Prevent Black-Asian Tensions," **The Wall Street Journal,** October 21, 1992.

*   *   *

Response Request

We appreciate your interest in *MULTICULTURAL COMMUNICATION STRATEGIES* and would like to know how it has been useful for you.

Are you primarily interested in:

Customers?   _____
Colleagues?   _____
Community?   _____
International?   _____
All the above?   _____

What sections of the book did you like best, and why.

_____
_____
_____
_____
_____
_____
_____
_____
_____
_____

In future editions, what areas would you like to see expanded. Examples of application would be helpful.

_____
_____
_____
_____
_____
_____

Any other comments.

_____
_____
_____
_____
_____
_____

May we quote you? Yes _____   No _____

For more information about multicultural products and services, please complete the following:

Name:_____Title:_____
Organization:_____
Address:_____
City:_____St:_____Zip:_____
Telephone:_____

Send this form to:

THE STARKEY GROUP, INC.
Tel: 773 348 0421

3180 N Lake Shore Drive, #17G
Chicago, IL 60657-4831

THANK YOU!